AFGHANS
TRADITIONAL
AND MODERN

by BONITA BRAY
Fashion Editor of Spinnerin Yarn Co., Inc.

CROWN PUBLISHERS, INC., NEW YORK

LIBRARY OF CONGRESS CATALOGING IN PUBLICATION DATA

Bray, Bonita.
  Afghans.

  Includes index.
  1. Knitting. 2. Crocheting. I. Title.
TT825.B7   1977   746.9   77-8641
ISBN 0-517-53104-6
ISBN 0-517-53105-4 pbk.

Designed by Rhea Braunstein

Contents

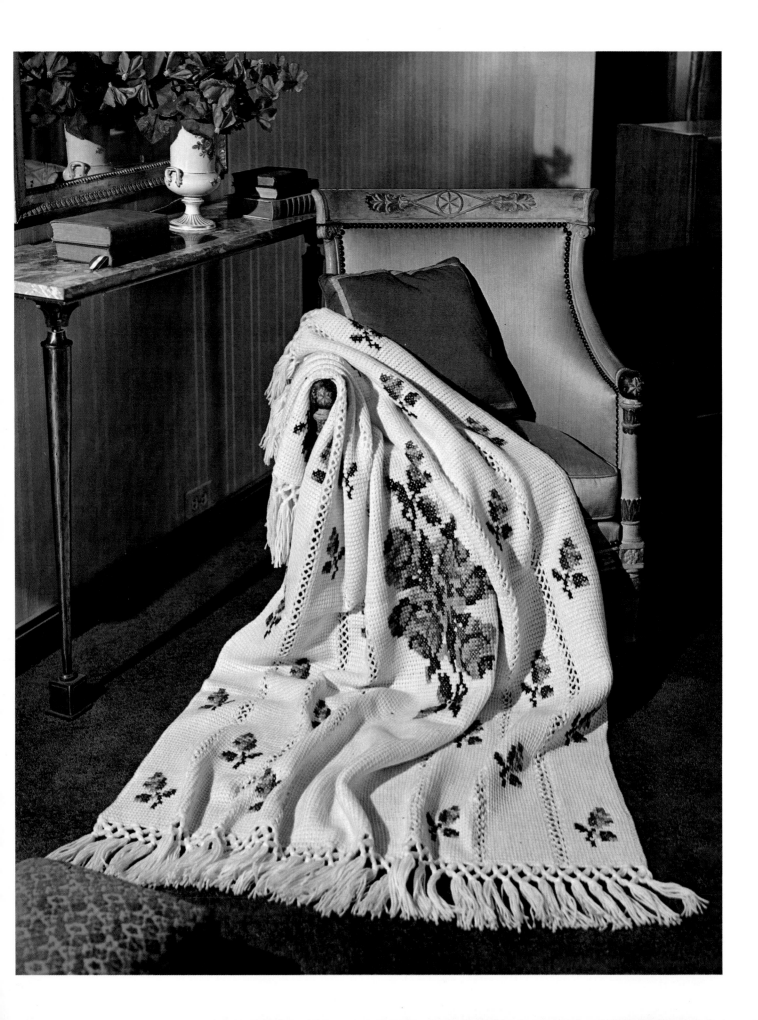

Introduction and Basic Stitches

Although afghans as we know them have been with us for many years, it is only recently that such a variety and so many designs have been available. You will find in this book a collection of every type of afghan from the old favorites to the soon-to-be favorites in your basic weights of yarn. Not only are there the traditional groupings, but for the adventurous knitter eager to tackle and conquer, there is the group of collectible Irish Fisherman afghans. For those who want a modern up-to-date look there are many varieties as well as the special afghans created for special needs. In all, there are a multitude of ideas and suggestions for every afghan, and I hope you will enjoy working and watching your afghan grow as I have watched so many of mine.

So — just don't do something. Knit or crochet yourself a beautiful afghan!

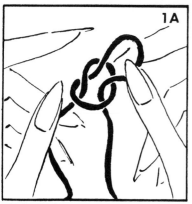

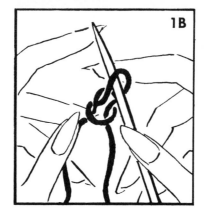

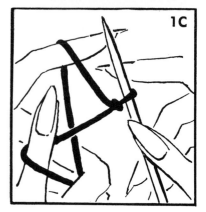

TO CAST ON

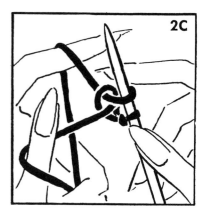

How to Knit

TO CAST ON: Allow 1 inch for each st. Make a loop (1A). Insert needle through loop (1B). Tighten loop. Wrap free end of yarn around left thumb to form loop and hold tightly between fingers of left hand. Place ball-yarn over index finger and under next 2 fingers (1C).

Then over-and-under little finger (for tension control). Insert needle through under side of loop on thumb (2A). Draw ball-yarn through (2B). Gently pull free end of yarn through with left hand to form st (2C). Repeat procedure.

TO KNIT

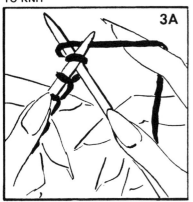

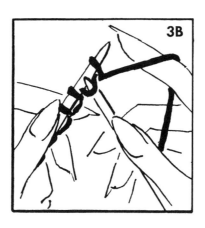

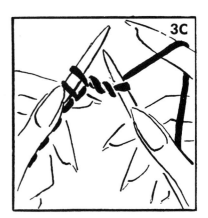

TO PURL

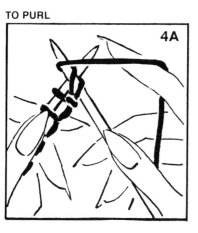

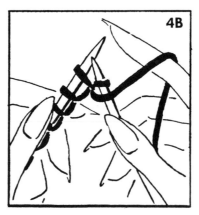

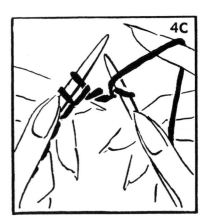

5A

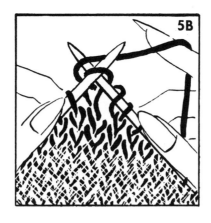

5B

6

YARN OVER BEFORE A KNIT STITCH

TO DECREASE

7A

7B

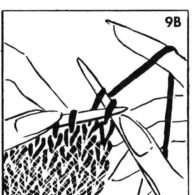

8

YARN OVER BEFORE A PURL STITCH

TO INCREASE

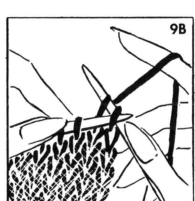

9A

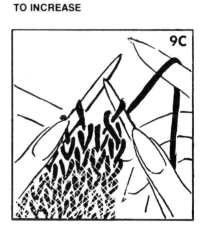

9B

9C

TO BIND OFF

TO KNIT: Hold needle with sts in left hand. Insert free needle in right hand through front of first st on left needle. Wrap yarn over point of right hand needle (3A). Draw yarn through (3B). Slip old st off left needle (3C). Repeat procedure.

TO PURL: Bring yarn to front of work. Insert right needle in front from right to left. Wrap yarn over needle (4A). Draw yarn through (4B). Slip old st off needle (4C). Repeat procedure.

YARN OVER BEFORE A KNIT STITCH: Bring yarn to front of needle (5A). Knit next stitch in usual manner (5B). An extra st has been added.

TO DECREASE: Knit 2 sts together (6). Or purl 2 sts together.

YARN OVER BEFORE A PURL STITCH: Wrap yarn completely around needle (7A). Then purl in usual manner (7B). An extra st has been added.

TO INCREASE: Knit into the front of the stitch in usual manner, but do not slip old st off needle. Then knit into the back of the same stitch (8). Now slip old st off needle.

TO BIND OFF: Knit 2 sts (9A). * Slip left hand needle into first st (9B), and slip first st over the second st (9C). Knit 1 st. Repeat from *. Break yarn. Draw through last stitch.

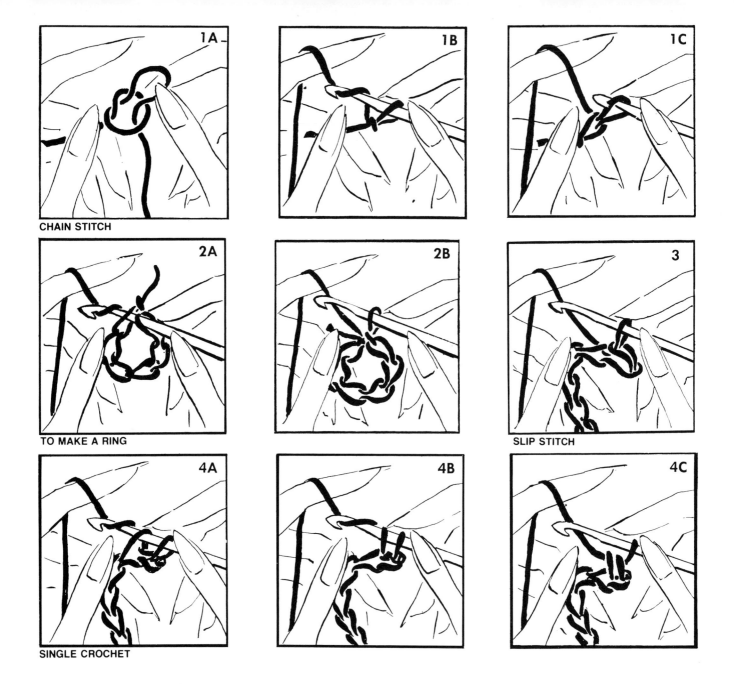

How to Crochet

CHAIN STITCH: Make a loop (1A). Wrap yarn around hook from back to front (1B). Draw yarn through (1C). Repeat.

TO MAKE A RING: Make several chain stitches. Insert hook in first chain. Wrap yarn over hook from back to front (2A). Draw yarn through chain and loop (2B).

SLIP STITCH: Skip first chain stitch. * Insert hook through st, wrap yarn over hook (1B), and draw loop through st and loop on hook (3). Repeat from *.

SINGLE CROCHET: Skip first chain. * Insert hook through st and wrap yarn over hook (4A). Draw loop through st—2 loops on hook (4B). Wrap yarn over hook and draw through 2 loops (4C). Repeat from *.

HALF DOUBLE CROCHET: Skip first chain. * Wrap yarn over hook (5A). Insert hook through next st, wrap yarn over hook and draw through st—3 loops on hook. Wrap yarn over hook (5B), and draw through 3 loops (5C). Repeat from *.

DOUBLE CROCHET: Skip first 2 ch. * Wrap yarn over hook (5A), insert in next st, wrap yarn over hook (6A). Draw loop through st—3 loops on hook. Wrap yarn over hook and draw through 2 loops—2 loops on hook (6B). Wrap yarn over hook and draw through 2 loops (6C). Repeat from *.

TREBLE CROCHET: Skip first 3 ch. ** Wrap yarn over hook twice (7A). Insert hook in next st, wrap yarn over hook and draw loop through st—4 loops on hook. *

8

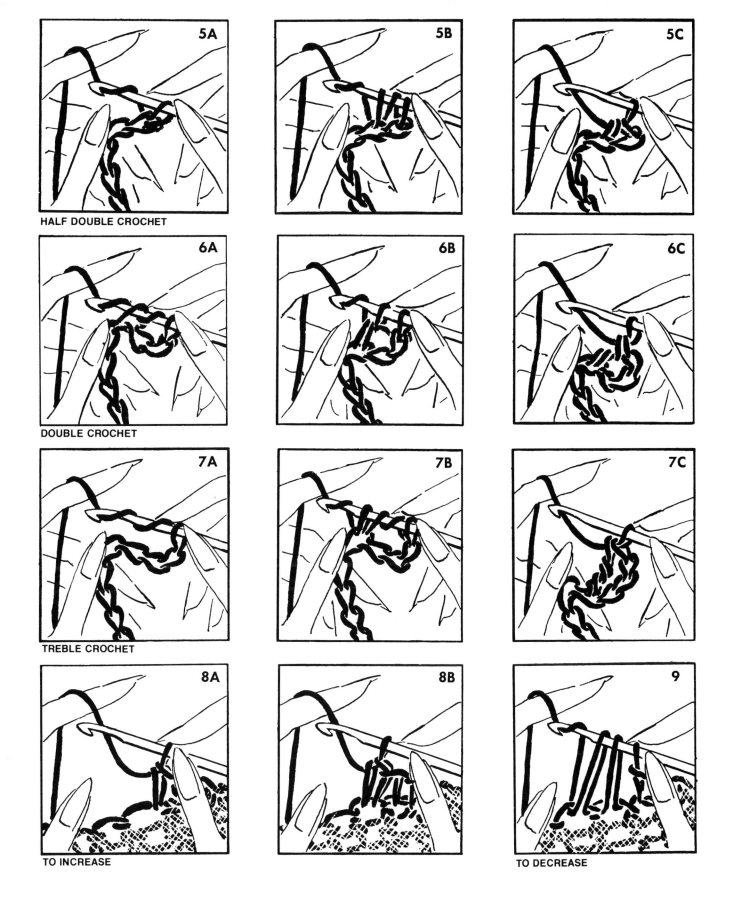

HALF DOUBLE CROCHET (5A, 5B, 5C)

DOUBLE CROCHET (6A, 6B, 6C)

TREBLE CROCHET (7A, 7B, 7C)

TO INCREASE (8A, 8B)

TO DECREASE (9)

Wrap yarn over hook (7B). Draw through 2 loops. Repeat from * 2 more times—1 loop on hook (7C). Repeat from * *

TO INCREASE: Make 1 st in usual manner (8A). Make a second stitch in same stitch (8B).

TO DECREASE: (a single crochet): Draw a loop through each of 2 sts (9). Wrap yarn over hook and draw through 3 loops. To decrease a dc, draw a loop through 2 sts, then complete in usual manner.

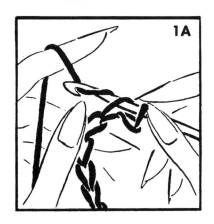

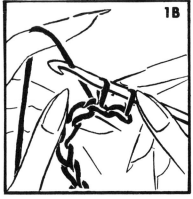

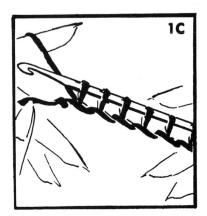

AFGHAN STITCH: ROW 1—FIRST HALF

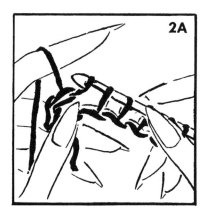

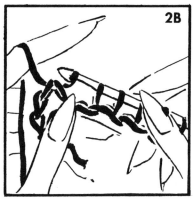

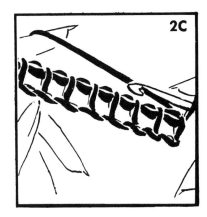

AFGHAN STITCH: ROW 1—SECOND HALF

How to Work the Basic Afghan Stitch

Work a chain of specified length.

Row 1—First Half: Skip chain from hook. * Insert hook through top loop only of next chain. Yarn over hook (1A). Draw yarn through chain, forming loop on hook. Retain loop on hook (1B). Rep from * across chain (1C). There will be the same number of loops on hook as number of chains.

Row 1—Second Half: Yarn over hook and draw through first loop (2A). * Yarn over and draw through 2 loops (2B). Rep from * across row until there is 1 loop on hook (2C). This loop is first st for next row.

Row 2—First Half: Insert hook in 2nd upright st or vertical bar, yarn over hook, draw loop through bar, forming loop on hook (3A). Retain loop on hook. Continue drawing up a loop through each bar across row (3B and 3C).

Row 2—Second Half: Same as 2nd half of Row 1. Rep Row 2 for pattern.

TO BIND OFF: Slip st across row as follows: * Draw up loop in bar and through loop on hook. Repeat from * across. Break yarn and draw through last loop.

AFGHAN STITCH: ROW 2—FIRST HALF

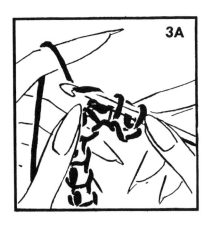

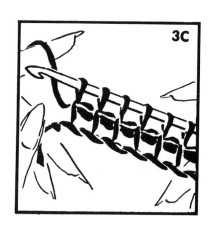

Afghan Stitch with Worked-in Patterns

These afghans are worked in one piece, following a chart. The stitch used is basic afghan stitch, changing colors according to chart.

TO FOLLOW CHART: On all rows, read chart from right to left. Remember that both halves of 1 row afghan st = 1 row on chart.

JOINING COLORS: On first half of row pick up the designated number of loops of first color shown on chart, join next color, pick up specified number of loops in this color, etc. When the same color appears with no more than 3 stitches of another color between, the first ball may be carried across — but **never more than 3 sts.** Join new balls of same color if necessary.

On 2nd half of row, work off loops with matching color until there is one st left of the color, then change colors, picking up yarn to be used under color previously used, thus twisting colors to prevent hole in work. New color will be drawn through 1 loop of previous color and 1 loop of new color.

When a color is no longer needed, break off, leaving an end long enough to be woven in on the wrong side.

Various Methods of Fringing

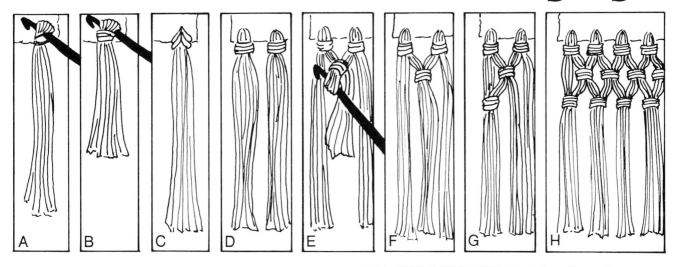

Use specific directions given with each afghan for the length to cut yarn, the number of strands and color to use and how to space.

Fold strands in half. Insert hook from wrong side and draw folds through.

Draw cut ends through folded loops.

FOR SINGLE KNOT FRINGE: Follow illustrations A through D.

FOR DOUBLE KNOT FRINGE: Follow illustrations A through F.

FOR TRIPLE KNOT FRINGE: Follow illustrations A through H.

Cross Stitch on Afghan Stitch

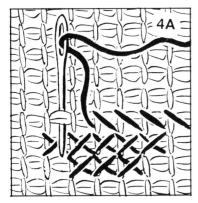
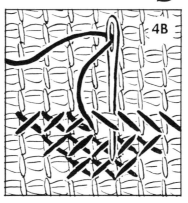
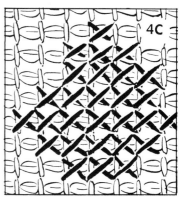

The Twist Stitches

There are many different ways of doing "Right" and "Left Twists," but the same abbreviations (RT and LT) are always used, regardless of the number of stitches being twisted. (Twist stitches are not the same as Cable stitches.) In each set of instructions, full details are given as to how each twist is worked in that particular pattern. To understand how to work these various twists, study the diagrams carefully.

Right Twist—A

Sk 1 st, K next st through front loop and leave on left needle (arrow shows how right needle is inserted—and note that right needle remains on **top** of left needle).

Shows yarn drawn through st. K the skipped st (instructions will specify whether through front or back loop) and drop 2 from left needle. (As you K the skipped st, pull both original sts from left needle and the 2 twisted sts are now on the right needle.)

Right Twist—B

Sk 1 st, K next st and leave on left needle (right needle is inserted through st to back of work, remaining **under** the left needle) K skipped st and drop 2 from needle (see Right Twist—A).

Diagram shows how a Right Twist looks when completed.

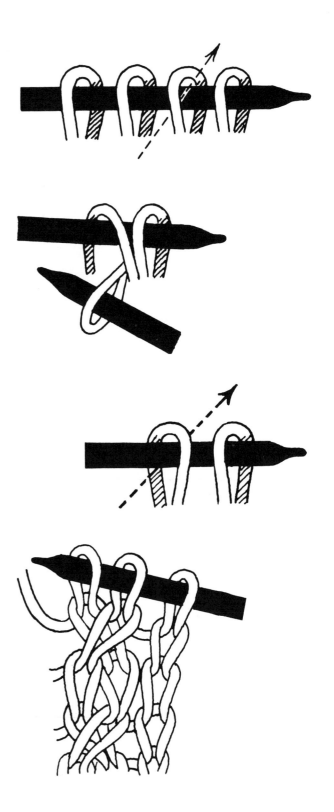

For additional examples see page 41.

HOW TO MAKE A POMPON

Step 1 — Cut 2 cardboard circles 1½ inch diameter for small; 2 inches diameter for medium and 3 inches for large pompon. Cut hole in middle of circles. Cut strands of yarn 6 yds. long.

Step 2 — Thread cut ends into blunt tapestry needle. Place circles tog. Draw needle through center over circles, and through loop formed by fold. Continue to wrap yarn over circles until yarn fills center hole and circles are completely covered.

Step 3 — With sharp scissors cut between circles at outside edge.

Step 4 — Wind 2 strands yarn about 8 inches long between circles, tie securely.

Step 5 — Remove circles. Attach pompons with yarn used for tying. Trim pompon evenly.

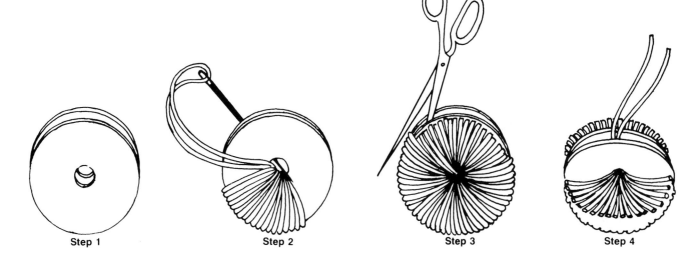

| Step 1 | Step 2 | Step 3 | Step 4 |

BACKWARD SINGLE CROCHET

You will often find this used as an edging. This simply means that a row of single crochet is worked from left to right (instead of the usual manner of right to left). Do not turn at end of last row, but always chain 1. Insert hook in last stitch of last row and work a single crochet, * insert hook in next stitch to right and work a single crochet; rep from * to end.

TO MAKE A TASSEL

Wrap yarn around a cardboard of given measurements the number of times specified. Cut yarn at 1 end. Remove 1 strand. Fold remaining strands in half over the strands removed. Wrap another strand tightly several times around folded strands 1 inch from fold, tie ends and draw to middle of tassel.

TO MAKE A TWISTED CORD

Cut strands of yarn 3 times desired length of cord. Tie ends tog forming 2 looped ends. Slide a pencil through each looped end. Have two people hold pencils. Keeping yarn taut, twist pencils in opposite directions. When yarn is tight and begins to kink, catch center of cord over a doorknob. Bring pencils together, allowing yarn to twist. If necessary run hand down twisted cord to smooth.

13

Section 1.
Modern Afghans

Although knitting and crocheting begins with a foundation fabric, many different directions are taken in this section of modern afghan designs. These afghans, in harmony with the decor of chrome and modern everyday needs, can be used as lap warmers, knee warmers, or body warmers. Created in bright bold colors, they fill every nook and cranny.

1.
Spanish Motif Afghan

Approximate Size: 62 × 85 inches

MATERIALS: Knitting Worsted Weight (4-oz.), 12 skeins White, 11 skeins Black, 4 skeins Red

AFGHAN HOOK: Size G **OR SIZE TO GIVE GAUGE**

GAUGE: 4 sts = 1 inch
15 rows = 4 inches

NOTE: Afghan panels are worked in Basic Afghan st and then cross stitched when completed following charts.

WHITE PANEL (Make 4): With hook chain 42. Work in Basic Afghan st for 310 rows. Bind off.

BLACK PANEL (Make 3): With hook chain 24. Work in Basic Afghan st for 310 rows. Bind off.

CROSS ST WHITE PANELS: Cross st White panels following Chart 1 working 2 rows plain at each end of pattern. Work from A to C; rep from B to C, 5 times more, work from B to A.

CROSS ST BLACK PANELS: Cross st Black panels beg at 7th row from bottom, * (work Chart 2, then sk 6 rows) 5 times, * (work Chart 2, then sk 7 rows) 2 times; rep between *'s once, work Chart 2. 8 sts remain. Work 2 panels in this way, then work 3rd panel beg at 8th row from bottom, leaving 7 sts at top.

FINISHING: With Black and wrong sides tog, sc panels tog.

BORDER: From wrong side, join Black at any corner to beg side edge, * 3 sc in corner, * ch 1, sk 1 row, 1 sc in next row; rep from * to 2 sts before corner, ch 1, sk 1 row, 3 sc in corner st; repeat from * around (sk sts or rows), join with a sl st to first sc. Ch 1, turn.

Rnd 2: Work 1 sc in each sc and sp around, working 3 sc at corners. Join. Ch 3, turn.

Rnd 3: In *Back* lps, * dc in each sc to corner, 5 dc in corner; rep from * around. Join with a sl st to first dc. Ch 1, turn.

Rnd 4: Inserting hook in *back* lp of dc and in free lp *of sc directly below*, sc to 5-dc corner, sc in back lp of next dc and in free lp of corner sc, (sc in back lp of next dc and in lp of same sc) 3 times more; rep from * around. Fasten off.

Rnd 5: Turn. Join Red in any corner st, * ch 1, sk 1 st, 1 sc in next st; rep from * around working 3 sc in each corner. Fasten off. Rep from Rnd 2 once. Rep Rnd 2 once more. Fasten off.

CHART 1 (Wide White Panel)

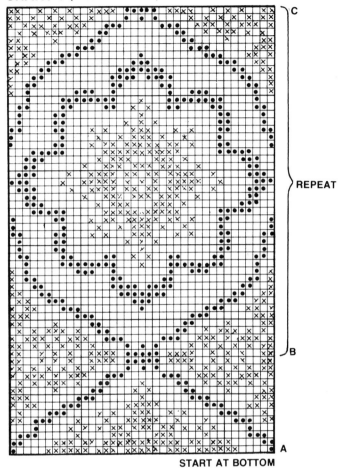

C

REPEAT

B

A

START AT BOTTOM

CHART 2 (Narrow Black Panel)

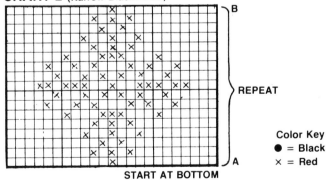

B

REPEAT

A

START AT BOTTOM

Color Key
● = Black
× = Red

2.
Red and White Circles Afghan

Approximate Size: 45 × 67 inches

MATERIALS: Knitting Worsted Weight (4-oz.), 7 skeins Red, 4 skeins White

AFGHAN HOOK: Size J **OR SIZE TO GIVE GAUGE**

GAUGE: 4 sts = 1 inch
3 rows = 1 inch

Afghan is worked in one piece in basic afghan stitch with worked in pattern.

With Red, chain 162 sts. Work 18 rows.

Row 19—Begin Chart: Work 15 border sts in Red, begin chart, work 66 sts, then work same 66 sts in reverse from left to right, work 15 border sts.

LENGTH: Work 89 rows of chart, then following chart, work 89 rows back to beg. Work 18 rows Red, bind off.

BORDER: From right side with hook and White, work 1 sc in each st around working 3 sc in corners, join. Rep rnd with Red, fasten off.

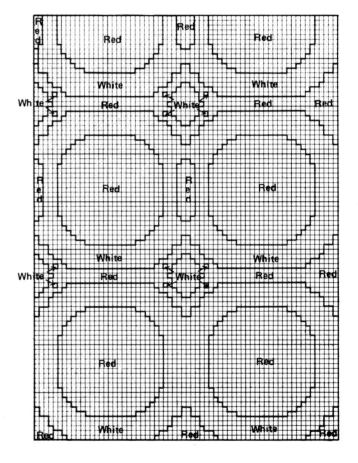

3.
Geometric Indian Afghan

Approximate Size: 51 × 72 inches (without fringe)

MATERIALS: Knitting Worsted Weight (4-oz.), 3 skeins each Black, Red, Unscoured White; 2 skeins Yellow; 1 skein each Orange, Gray, Hunter, Loden

AFGHAN HOOK: Size J Flexible **OR SIZE TO GIVE GAUGE**

GAUGE: 4 sts = 1 inch
3 rows = 1 inch

NOTE: Afghan is worked in Basic Afghan st with worked in pattern. With Black chain 196 sts. Work 3 rows Black, 1 row Gray, 1 row White, 1 row Gray, 1 row Black, 2 rows Yellow, 2 rows Orange, 2 rows Red.

Row 14: Work 10 sts Red, begin chart, work chart to end, work 10 sts Red. Keeping 10 sts in Red at each end, work to end of chart, then rep from * to **, work 2

rows Red, 2 rows Orange, 2 rows Yellow, 1 row Black, 1 row Gray, 1 row White, 1 row Gray, 3 rows Black. Bind off, do *not* fasten off.

FINISHING: With Black, ch 3, dc in same sp, * sk 1 st, ch 1, work 2 dc in next st (puff st); rep from * across adjusting to end puff st in last st. Ch 3, turn.

Row 2: Puff st in first ch-1 sp and in each ch-1 sp across, ending puff st in Tch. Ch 3, turn.

Row 3: Rep Row 2. Fasten off.

Join yarn on opposite end and work in same way.

FRINGE: Wrap yarn around a 6-inch cardboard. Cut at one end. With 3 strands, insert hook from wrong side in first ch-1 sp, draw fold through, draw cut ends through fold. Knot a 3-strand fringe in each ch-1 sp on each end. Trim.

Chart Shows Center 176 Stitches

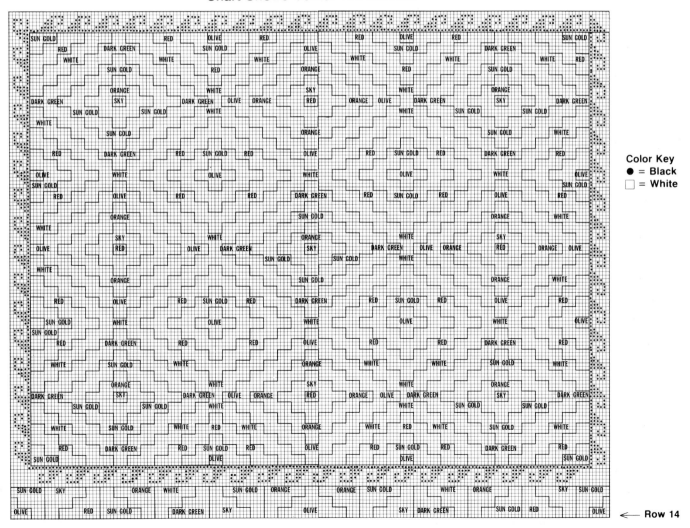

Color Key
● = Black
□ = White

← Row 14

4.
Popcorn Square Afghan

Approximate Size: 60 × 75 inches

MATERIALS: Knitting Worsted Weight (4-oz.), 35 skeins

NEEDLES: No. 11 **OR SIZE TO GIVE GAUGE**

GAUGE: 1 square = 15 × 15 inches
16 sts = 5 inches
20 rows = 5 inches

NOTE: Afghan squares are worked with 2 strands of yarn held together.

TO MAKE POPCORN: In next st, K 1 in front lp, (K 1 on back lp, K 1 on front lp) twice (5 sts in 1 st), turn; P 5, turn; K 5, turn; P 5, turn; K 5, sl the 2nd, 3rd, 4th and 5th st on right needle over the first st (Popcorn st—**PO**).

SQUARES—Make 20: Cast on 49 sts. K 2 rows.

Row 3: K 2, (Garter st), *PO, K 3; rep from *, end **PO**, K 2 (Garter st).

Row 4: K 2, P to last 2 sts, K 2.

Row 5: Knit.

Row 6: K 2, P to last 2 sts, K 2.

Row 7: Rep Row 3.

Row 8 through 10: Rep Rows 4 through 6.

Row 11: K 2, **PO**, K 3, **PO**, K to last 7 sts, **PO**, K 3, **PO**, K 2.

Rows 12 through 14: Rep Rows 4 through 6.

Rep from Row 11 twice.

Row 23: K 2, **PO**, K 3, **PO**, K 11; **PO**, (K 3, **PO**) 3 times; K 11; **PO**; K3, **PO**; K 2.

Rows 24 through 26: Rep Rows 4 through 6.

Rep from Row 23 4 times. (5 **PO** rows in center.)

Row 42: Rep Row 11.

Rows 43 through 65: Rep Rows 22 through Row 1. Bind off as to K.

FINISHING: Holding wrong sides tog and matching sts, overcast edges of squares tog, forming strips of 5 squares for length. (Overcast 4 strips tog for width.)

FRINGE: Wrap yarn around an 8-inch cardboard and cut at 1 end. Fold 6 strands in half. Insert hook from wrong side in first st on 1 end, draw fold through, draw cut ends through fold. Place fringe in every end st on both ends.

NOTE: For Popcorn Stitch
Chevron Afghan instructions,
see page 71.

22

5.
Nautical Afghan
(Shown on opposite page at top left)

Approximate Size: 48 × 66 inches (without fringe)

MATERIALS: (Knitting Worsted Weight (4-oz.), 5 White, 3 each Yellow, Blue, Red and 1 Black

AFGHAN HOOK: 14-inch or Flexible Size H **OR SIZE TO GIVE GAUGE**

GAUGE: 4 sts = 1 inch
3 rows = 1 inch

NOTE: Afghan is worked in 1 piece in afghan stitch with worked-in pattern.

It is of prime importance that you work to the gauge given above, otherwise your afghan will not be the measurements given and the design will not be as shown.
With colors as shown on Row 1 of chart, ch 192 to measure 48 inches. Follow chart for 196 rows. Bind off.

FINISHING: Sew in end. Block. With Black and using outline stitch, work horizontal then vertical lines to separate flags.

BORDER: With Black from right side, work sc on edges of afghan, spacing sts to keep edges flat and working 3 sc at corners. Join with a sl st, ch 1.

Row 2: Sc in each sc, 3 sc at corners. Join and fasten off.

FRINGE: Wrap White around a 24-inch cardboard. Cut at 1 end. Fold 2 strands in half. Insert hook from wrong side in first st on short end, draw fold through, draw cut ends through fold. Knot fringe in each st across both ends.

Tie 2 adjoining grps, of 8 fringes each, into a square knot as shown. There will be 12 square knots at each end. Trim evenly.

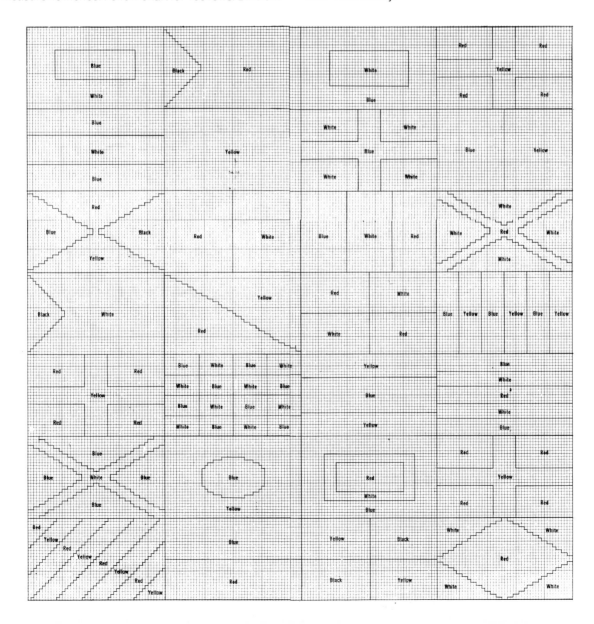

6.
Green and White Snowflake Afghan

Approximate Size: 60 × 64 inches (without fringe)

MATERIALS: Knitting Worsted Weight (4-oz.), 8 MC and 6 CC

AFGHAN HOOK: 14-inch or Flexible Size H **OR SIZE TO GIVE GAUGE**

GAUGE: 4 sts = 1 inch
4 rows = 1 inch

NEEDLES: No. 8 **OR SIZE TO GIVE GAUGE**

GAUGE: 5 sts = 1 inch
6 rows = 1 inch

HOOK: Size H

AFGHAN STITCH CC PANELS (Make 4): With Afghan Hook, chain 21.

Row 1—First Half: Insert hook in top lp of first st from hook, draw yarn through and retain lp on hook; * insert hook in top lp of next ch, draw yarn through and retain lp on hook; rep from * to end. 21 lps.

Row 1—Second Half: Yo and through one lp, * yo and through 2 lps; rep from * to end. One lp remains and is the first st of next row.

Row 2—First Half: Sk end st, * insert hook under next bar, draw yarn through and retain lp on hook; rep from * to end. 21 lps.

Row 2—Second Half: Same as 2nd half of Row 1.

Rep Row 2 for pat and work total of 256 rows. Bind off by * inserting hook in next bar and draw yarn through bar and lp on hook; rep from * to end. Fasten off last lp.

FINISHING: With MC, Cross st 6 snowflakes, following chart.
Beg. on 23rd row, center design and work the 17 rows of design. Sk 22 rows between snowflakes.

KNIT MC PANELS (Make 5): With MC and No. 8 needles, cast on 29 sts.

Row 1 (right side): P 1, * K 6, P 1; rep from * to end.

Row 2: K 1, * P 6, K 1; rep from * to end.

Row 3: P 1, * K 2, sl next 2 as to P, K 2, P 1; rep from * to end.

Row 4: K 1, * P 2, sl next 2 as to P, P 2, K 1; rep from * to end.

Row 5: P 1, * sl next 2 sts to dp needle and hold at back, K next st, K 2 sts from dp needle; sl next st to dp needle and hold at front, K next 2 sts, K st from dp, P 1; rep from * to end. Rep from Row 2 for pat until same length as CC panels, ending with Pat Row 4, bind off.

SIDE EDGING—CC PANELS: With CC and crochet hook, sc in corner, * ch 5, sk 1 row, sc in next row; rep from * to end. Fasten off. 128 lps. Work other side of panel to correspond.

TO JOIN MC PANEL: With MC and from right side of MC panel, sc in corner, ch 2, sc in first CC ch-5 (hold wrong sides of panels tog), * ch 2, sk 2 rows on MC panel, sc in next row, ch 2, sc in next CC ch-5; rep from * ending with sc in last MC row and all lps joined. Fasten off. Join all panels in this way.

FINISHING—Side Edges: With MC from wrong side, work sc along side, spacing sts to keep edge flat. Ch 1, turn.

SHELL ROW: Sc in first sc, * sk 2 sc, 5 dc in next sc, sk 2 sc, sc in each of next 2 sc; rep from * to end.

With MC, work 2 rows sc along top and bottom edges.

FRINGE: Wrap yarn around a 9-inch cardboard and cut at one end. Knot fringes over sc row, MC over MC panels, CC over CC panels, in first and every 3rd st. Fold 4 strands in half, insert hook from wrong side, draw fold through, draw cut ends through fold and tighten on right side. Trim evenly.

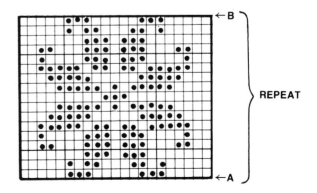

7.
Geometric Afghan

Approximate Size: 68 × 70 inches

MATERIALS: Knitting Worsted Weight (4-oz.), 3 Yellow (Y), 4 Aqua (A), 5 Red (R) and 6 Navy (N)

CROCHET HOOK: Size I **OR SIZE TO GIVE GAUGE**

GAUGE: 7 sc = 2 inches
4 rows = 1 inch

NOTE: It is advisable to block afghan at suggested intervals. To block, pin afghan to a padded surface, steam and allow to dry before continuing work. Entire afghan is worked in single crochet.

To change colors: Work last sc of a color to last step, drop color and cut. Draw new color through 2 lps on hook.

AFGHAN

With Y chain 5 for center of afghan. Join with a sl st to first ch to form a ring.

Rnd 1: Work 8 sc in ring. Do *not* join. Mark end of every rnd.

Rnd 2: 2 sc in each sc. 16 sc.

Rnd 3: * Sc in 1 sc, 2 sc in next sc; rep from * around. 24 sc.

Rnd 4: * Sc in each of 2 sc, 2 sc in next sc; rep from * around. 32 sc.

Rnd 5: Sc in each sc.

Continue this way to inc 8 sc every 2nd rnd, having 1 st more between incs in every inc rnd until there are 18 rnds from beg and 88 sc in rnd. Do *not* complete last sc of rnd. Drop Y and cut. Draw R through lps on hook.

Rnd 19—Work with R to form square as follows: Sc in each of 10 sc, 3 sc in next sc (corner), * sc in each of next 21 sc, 3 sc in next sc (corner); rep from * twice more, sc in each of last 11 sc. 4 corners, 96 sc.

Rnd 20: * Sc in each sc to center sc of corner, 3 sc in center sc; rep from * 3 times more, sc in each sc to end of rnd. 104 sc. Rep last rnd 25 times more completing last sc of rnd. There are 75 sc on each side and 4 corner sts. (304 sts). Form triangles as follows: Join A from right side in first sc to left of corner sc.

Row 1: Draw up a lp in same sc with joining, draw up a lp in next sc, yo and through 3 lps on hook (1 sc dec), sc in each sc to 2 sc before corner, dec 1 sc. Ch 1, turn at end of every row.

Row 2: Dec 1 sc each side as before.

Continue to dec 1 sc each side *every* row until there are 3 sc in last row.

Next Row: Draw up a lp in each of 3 sc, yo and through 4 lps on hook (dec). Ch 1 and fasten off.

2nd Triangle: Skip the corner sc at end of first row of first triangle and join A in first sc. Work same as first triangle.

Work triangle on other 2 sides of square in same way.

Form square around a triangle as follows: Join N in free R sc of any corner, sc in same place with joining and in each of 37 A rows to top of triangle, 3 sc in dec at top of triangle (corner), * sc in end of each A row to next R corner st, sc in corner st, sc in each row of next A triangle; rep from *, end sc in end of each 37 A rows. 77 sc on each side and 4 corner sts (312 sts). Work 15 rnds of 1 sc in each sc, 3 sc in center sc of each corner. Join with a sl st to first sc of last rnd and fasten off. 107 sc on each side and 4 corner sts (432 sts).

IT IS ADVISABLE TO BLOCK AFGHAN AT THIS POINT

Work with R to form stripe on edges of square as follows:
Join R from right side in first sc to left of center sc at corner.

Row 1: Same as Row 1 to form a triangle.

Row 2: SC in each sc, ch 1, turn.

Dec 1 st each side every 2nd row until there are 16 R rows, do *not* complete last sc of last row. Cut R draw Y through. Ch 1, turn. Work with Y to form stripe as follows: Dec 1 st each side every 2nd row until there are 16 Y rows. 75 sc in last row. Draw A through lp on hook, cut Y. Ch 1, turn.

Continue triangle as follows: Always drop yarn not in use to *front* of work and do *not* cut.

Row 1: Dec 1 sc, sc in each of next 11 sc working off last sc with R; sc in each of next 12 sc, working off last sc with Y; sc in each of next 25 sc, working off last sc with 2nd ball R, sc in next 12 sc, working off last sc with A; sc in each of next 11 sc, dec 1 sc. Ch 1, turn.

Row 2: Matching colors, work sc in each sc. Ch 1, turn.

Row 3: Work as in Row 1, having same number sc in A and R sections and 2 sc less in Y section.

Rep last 2 rows until there are 15 sc in Y section. Work 1 row even.

Next Row: Work as Row 3, replacing Y with N.

Continue as in rows 2 and 3 until there is 1 sc in center N section. Work 1 row even. Fasten off N.

Next Row: Sc in each sc to R, dec, work to N st (center st), work R in center st, work to 2 sts before A, dec, sc in each sc to end.

Continue as in Rows 2 and 3 until 1 R st remains. Work 1 row even. Continue as in Rows 2 and 3 with A until 1 st remains. Fasten off. Work on other 3 sides of N square in same way.

IT IS AGAIN ADVISABLE TO BLOCK AFGHAN AT THIS POINT

Work with N to form border as follows: Join N in *free* sc of any N square corner.

Rnd 1: Sc in same st with joining, sc in each row on side edge to single A sc at point, * in point work sc, ch 3, sc (corner); sc in each row to next *free* sc of N square, sc in N, sc in each row to next A point; rep from * around, sc in each sc to beg of rnd.

Rnd 2: Sc in each sc to point, * sc in ch-3 of previous row, ch 3, sc in same ch-3, sc in each sc to point; rep from * around, ending sc in each sc to beg of rnd. Rep last rnd 14 times more. Join with a sl st to first sc. Fasten off.

LAY AFGHAN ON A FLAT SURFACE AND STEAM

TASSELS (Make 4): Hold two 12 inch strands N at top of a 10-inch cardboard, then wrap 2 strands 25 times over cardboard. Tie 2 strands tightly tog at center over wrapped strands and knot securely. Cut at opposite end. Wind a 6-inch strand tightly around wrapped strands 1 inch from top and knot. Draw ends into center of tassel. Cut lower ends and trim. Using top strands, join a tassel to ch-3 at corners.

Section 2.
Irish Fisherman Afghans

For hundreds of years the fishermen of the British Isles have gone to sea wearing guernseys and jerseys with the individual designs of their villages. Here are many of those pattern stitches collected together in the form of the afghan. The lovely intertwining of cables, most of which have names, will make an interesting conversation piece for years to come.

8.
Shannon

Approximate Size: 52 × 68 inches

MATERIALS: Knitting Worsted Weight (4-oz.), 12 skeins.

NEEDLES: No. 10 **OR SIZE TO GIVE GAUGE**
1 dp or cable needle

HOOK: Size F
Large Eye Tapestry Needle

GAUGE: Each motif is 8½ inches square

Afghan is worked in 48 squares.

STITCHES

BACK CABLE (BC): Sl next 2 sts to dp needle and hold at *back*, K next 2 sts, K 2 from dp.

FRONT CABLE (FC): Sl next 2 sts to dp needle and hold at *front*, K next 2 sts, K 2 from dp.

TWIST 2 (T2): Sk 1 st, K next st through *front* loop and leave on left needle, K skipped st, drop 2 sts from left needle.

LEFT TWIST (LT): Sk 1 st, P next st through *back* loop and leave on left needle, K skipped st, drop 2 sts from left needle.

RIGHT TWIST (RT): Sk 1 st, K next st, P the skipped st.

BOBBLE (BO): K next st, leave on left needle, yo, pass last st on right needle over the yo, (K the worked st on left needle, leave on left needle, yo, pass last st on right needle over yo) twice, K in back loop of worked st on left needle, drop st from left needle, pass 3 sts on right needle over the last st on right needle.

MOTIF (Make 48): Cast on 41 sts. K 2 rows.
Row 1 (right side): K 1, P 1, K 8, P 2, **T2,** P 3, K 1, P 5, K 1, P 3, P 12, K 2.

Row 2: K 2, place a marker on needle; (on front loop of next st K 1, P 1, K 1; P next 3 sts tog) 3 times; place a marker on needle, K 3, P 1, K 5, P 1, K 3, P 2, K 2, P 8, K 2. Sl markers every row.

Row 3: K 1, P 1, (**BC**) twice, P 2, **T2,** P 3, K 1, P 5, K 1, P 3, P 12, K 2.

Row 4: K 2, (P 3 tog, work 3 sts in next st) 3 times, K 3, P 1, K 5, P 1, K 3, P 2, K 2, P 8, K 2.

Row 5: K 1, P 1, K 8, P 2, **T2,** P 3, **LT,** P 3, **RT,** P 3, P 12, K 2.

Row 6: K 2; rep between markers of Row 2, K 4, P 1, K 3, P 1, K 4, P 2, K 2, P 8, K 2.

Row 7: K 1, P 1, K 2, **FC,** K 2, P 2, **T2,** P 4, **LT,** P 1, **RT,** P 4, P 12, K 2.

Row 8: K 2, rep betwen markers of Row 4, K 5, P 1, K 1, P 1, K 5, P 2, K 2, P 8, K 2.

Row 9: K 1, P 1, K 8, P 2, **T2,** P 2, **BO,** P 2, sl next st to dp needle, hold at *front*, **RT,** K st from dp, P 2, **BO,** P 2, P 12, K 2.

Row 10: K 2; rep between markers of Row 2, K 2, P 1, K 2, P 3, K 2, P 1, K 2, P 2, K 2, P 8, K 2.
Rep these 10 rows (taking care to alternate sts between markers on every wrong side row) until there are 40 rows in pat. P 1 row on right side. Bind off.

FINISHING: Block each square lightly to measure 8½ inches square. Check photograph for the position of squares, and weave together from the right side. Join 6 squares, in width, 8 squares in length. On side edges, from right side, work 1 row sc, ch 1, do not turn. Work 2nd row from left to right (backward crochet) and fasten off.

KNITTED FRINGE (Make 2 strips): With 2 strands of yarn held tog, cast on 8 sts.

Row 1: Yo (wrap yarn around right needle), P 2 tog, (yo, P 2 tog) 3 times. Rep Row 1 until same length as lower edge of afghan.

Next Row: Work 6 sts and drop last 2 sts from left needle without working (to form loops when raveled). Turn and bind off 6 sts loosely. Pin long side (opposite fringe) to edge of afghan and weave in same manner as with squares. Ravel fringe and steam lightly. Do not cut.

9.
Limerick

Approximate Size: 57 × 66 inches plus fringe

MATERIALS: Knitting Worsted Weight (4-oz.), 14 skeins

NEEDLES: No. 10 **OR SIZE TO GIVE GAUGE**
2 dp or cable needles

HOOK: Size G

GAUGE: 1 Strip (60 Sts) = 11½ inches
11 rows = 2 inches

Afghan is worked in 5 panels.

PATTERN 1: Worked on 18 sts.
Row 1 (right side): P 2, (K 6, P 2) twice.

Row 2: K 2, (P 6, K 2) twice.
Row 3: P 2, (sl next 2 sts to dp needle, hold at *back* of work, K next st, K 2 from dp, sl next st to dp, hold at *front* of work, K next 2 sts, K st from dp, P 2) twice.

Row 4: Rep Row 2.
Rep these 4 rows for Pat 1.

STITCHES FOR PAT 2

CROSS ON 8 STS: Sl next 2 sts to dp and hold at *front*, sl next 4 sts to 2nd dp and hold at *back*, K next 2 sts, K 4 from 2nd dp, K 2 from the first dp.

RIGHT TWIST (RT): Sl next 2 sts to dp and hold at *back*, K next 2 sts, P 2 from dp.

LEFT TWIST (LT): Sl next 2 sts to dp and hold at *front*, P next 2 sts, K 2 from dp.

PATTERN 2: Worked on 24 sts.

Row 1 (right side): P 8, K 8, P 8.

Rows 2 and 4: K 8, P 8, K 8.

Row 3: P 8, **CROSS 8**, P 8.

Row 5: P 6, **RT**, K 4, **LT**, P 6.

Row 6: K 6, P 2, K 2, P 4, K 2, P 2, K 6.

Row 7: P 4, **RT**, P 2, K 4, P 2, **LT**, P 4.

Row 8: K 4, P 2, K 4, P 4, K 4, P 2, K 4.

Row 9: (P 2, **RT**) twice, (**LT**, P 2) twice.

Row 10: K 2, (P 2, K 4) 3 times, P 2, K 2.

Row 11 (RT, P 2) twice, (P 2, **LT**) twice.

Rows 12 and 14: P 2, K 4, P 2, K 8, P 2, K 4, P 2.

Row 13: K 2, P 4, K 2, P 8, K 2, P 4, K 2.

Rows 15 through 18: Rep Rows 13 and 14 twice.

Row 19: (**LT**, P 2) twice, (P 2, **RT**) twice.

Row 20: Rep Row 10.

Row 21: (P 2, **LT**) twice, (**RT**, P 2) twice.

Row 22: Rep Row 8.

Row 23: P 4, **LT**, P 2, K 4, P 2, **RT**, P 4.

Row 24: Rep Row 6.

Row 25: P 6, **LT**, K 4, **RT**, P 6.

Row 26: Rep Row 2.
Rep these 26 rows for Pat 2.

AFGHAN

PANELS (Make 5): Cast on 60 sts.
Row 1: Work first rows of Pat 1 over 18 sts; Pat 2 over 24 sts; Pat 1 over 18 sts. Keeping pats as established, work to approx 66 inches from beg, ending with Row 1 of Pat 1, Row 5 of Pat 2. Bind off in pat.

FINISHING: From right side, overcast panels tog. Steam seams.

BORDER: Working from right side, join yarn over first st at one end.

Row 1: Ch 3; (yo, draw up a 1½-inch loop in same place with joining) 3 times, yo and through 6 loops, yo and through 2 loops (puff st); * ch 1, sk 1 st, work puff st in next st; rep from * to end. Fasten off.

Row 2: Ch 3, puff st in sp between ch-3 of Row 1 and next puff st, puff st in each sp between puff sts. Fasten off.

FRINGE: Wrap yarn around a 6-inch cardboard and cut at one end. Using 3 strands, knot fringe between puff sts on ends.

10. Killarney

Approximate Size: 54 × 66 inches plus fringe

MATERIALS: Knitting Worsted Weight (4-oz.), 10 skeins

NEEDLES: 27-inch circular No. 10 **OR SIZE TO GIVE GAUGE**
2 dp or cable needles

GAUGE: 11 sts = 2 inches
       5 rows = 1 inch

Afghan is worked back and forth on circular needle in one piece.

STITCHES

RIGHT TWIST (RT): Sk next st, K next st through *front* loop and leave on left needle, K the skipped st, drop 2 from left needle.

CABLE BACK (CB): Sl next 2 sts to dp needle and hold at *back,* K next 2 sts, K 2, from dp.

CABLE FRONT (CF): Sl next 2 sts to dp needle and hold at *front,* K next 2 sts, K 2 from dp.

CABLE 8 (C8): Sl next 2 sts to dp needle and hold at *front,* sl next 4 sts to 2nd dp needle and hold at *back,* K next 2 sts, P 4 from 2nd dp, K 2 from first dp.

PATTERN 1: Worked on 48 sts.

Row 1: RT, P 2, **(CB, CF)** 5 times, P 2, **RT.**

Rows 2, 3 and 4: K the knit sts and P the purl sts.

Row 5: RT, P 2 **(CF, CB)** 5 times, P 2, **RT.**

Rows 6, 7 and 8: K the knit sts and P the purl sts. Rep these 8 rows for Pat 1.

PATTERN 2: Worked on 34 sts.

Row 1: P 2, (K 2, P 4, K 2, P 3) twice, K 2, P 4, K 2, P 2.

Row 2: K the knit sts and P the purl sts.

Rows 3 and 4: Rep Rows 1 and 2 .

Row 5: P 2, **C8,** P 3, K 2, P 4, K 2, P 3, **C8,** P 2.

Row 6: Rep Row 2.

Rows 7 through 10: Rep Rows 1 and 2 twice.

Row 11: Rep Row 5.

Row 12: Rep Row 2.

Rows 13 through 16: Rep Rows 1 and 2 twice.

Row 17: P 2, K 2, P 4, K 2, P 3, **C8,** P 3, K 2, P 4, K 2, P 2.

Row 18: Rep Row 2.

Rows 19 through 22: Rep Rows 1 and 2 twice.

Row 23: Rep Row 17.

Row 24: Rep Row 2.

Rep these 24 rows for Pat 2.

AFGHAN

Cast on 296 sts. P 1 row.

Row 1: K 1, (work first rows of Pat 1 over 48 sts; Pat 2 over 34 sts) 3 times, Pat 1 over 48 sts, K 1.
Keeping pats as established, work to approx 66 inches from beg, ending with Pat Row 16. Bind off in pat.

TASSEL FRINGE: Wrap yarn around a 10-inch cardboard and cut at one end. Using 8 strands, knot one fringe in first and last cast-on sts, then space fringes so there are a total of 9 across each 48 st panel, 6 across each 34 panel. Beg with the first 3 fringes, tie 3 tog across end. Fringe bound-off row the same.

11. Galway

Approximate Size: 50 × 62 inches plus fringe

MATERIALS: Knitting Worsted Weight (4-oz.), 17 skeins

NEEDLES: Size 11 **OR SIZE TO GIVE GAUGE**
1 dp or cable needle

HOOK: Size J

GAUGE: Side Panels = 16½ inches in width
Center Panel = 17½ inches in width
4 rows = 1 inch

Afghan is worked with double yarn in 3 panels.

STITCHES

CABLE FRONT (CF): Sl next 3 sts to dp needle and hold at *front*, K next 3 sts, K 3 from dp.

RIGHT TWIST (RT): Sk next st, K next st through *front* loop and leave on left needle, K skipped st, drop 2 sts from left needle.

LEFT TWIST (LT): Sk next st, K next st through *back* loop and leave on left needle, K skipped st, drop 2 from left needle.

PATTERN 1: Worked on 10 sts.

Row 1: P 2, **CF**, P 2.

Rows 2 through 6: K the knit sts and P the purl sts. Rep these 6 rows for Pat 1.

PATTERN 2: Worked on 44 sts.

Row 1: (RT, LT) 11 times.

Rows 2 and 4: Purl.

Row 3: (LT, RT) 11 times.
Rep these 4 rows for Pat 2.

SIDE PANELS: (make 2): Cast on 64 sts.

Row 1: Work first rows of Pat 1 over 10 sts, Pat 2 over 44 sts; Pat 1 over 10 sts.

Keeping pats as established, work 246 rows, ending with Pat Row 6 of Pat 1. Bind off in pat. Piece should measure approx 61½ inches. Bind off.

CENTER PANEL

PATTERN 3: Cast on 72 sts.

Row 1: K 1, * K 3, P 4, K 3; rep from *, ending K 1.

Row 2 and All Even-Numbered Rows: K the knit sts and P the purl sts.

Row 3: K 1, * sl next 3 sts to dp and hold at *front*, P 1, K 3 sts from dp; P 2, sl next st to dp and hold at *back*, K 3, P st from dp; rep from *, ending K 1.

Row 5: K 1, P 1, * sl next 3 sts to dp and hold at *front*, P 1, K 3 from dp; sl next st to dp and hold at *back*, K 3, P st from dp, P 2; rep from *, ending last rep P 1, K 1.

Row 7: K 1, P 2, * sl next 3 sts to dp and hold at *front*, K 3, K 3 from dp, P 4; rep from *, ending last rep P 2, K 1.

Row 9: K 1, P 1, * sl next st to dp and hold at *back*, K 3, P st from dp; sl next 3 sts to dp and hold at *front*, P 1, K 3 from dp, P 2; rep from *, ending last rep P 1, K 1.

Row 11: K 1, * sl next st to dp and hold at *back*, K 3, P st from dp; P 2, sl next 3 sts to dp and hold at *front*, P 1, K 3, from dp; rep from *, ending K 1.

Row 13: K 1, K 3, * P 4, sl next 3 sts to dp and hold at *back*, K 3, K 3 from dp; rep from *, ending last rep K 3, K 1.

Row 14: K the knit sts and P the Purl sts.
Rep these 14 rows for Pat 3 and work 246 rows, ending with Pat Row 8. Bind off in pat.

FINISHING: Weave panels tog.
Beg at cast on row from right side, work 1 sc in each cast on st, 3 sc at corner; sc on side edge, spacing sts to keep edge flat, 3 sc at corner; continue sc on other edges in same way, ending 3 sc at corner; join with a sl st. Ch 3, turn. From right side, work 1 dc in each sc on ends only. Steam lightly.

FRINGE: Wrap yarn around an 8-inch cardboard and cut at one end. Using 6 strands, knot fringe in first and every 2nd dc on ends.

12.
Kilkenny

(Shown on left)

Approximate Size: 53 × 68 inches.

MATERIALS: Knitting Worsted Weight (4-oz.), 12 skeins

NEEDLES: Size 10 **OR SIZE TO GIVE GAUGE**
1 dp or cable needle

HOOK: Size G

GAUGE: 1 panel (34 sts) = 8½ inches
11 rows = 2 inches

Afghan is worked in 6 panels.

PANELS (Make 6): Cast on 34 sts.

Row 1 (wrong side): K 1, P 1, K 1, P 4, K 1, P 1 (Border); K 6, P 4, K 6; P 1, K 1, P 4, K 1, P 1, K 1 (Border).

Row 2: P1, * insert needle in center of next st in row below, K this st, leave st on left needle, K the same st on left needle, drop st from left needle, pass the 2nd st on right needle over first st on right needle **(Knit Twist— KT)**, P 1, K 4, P 1, **KT,** * P 6, sl next 2 sts to dp needle and hold at *back* of work, K next 2 sts, K 2 from dp needle **(Cable 4),** P 6; rep between *'s once, P 1.

Row 3: K 1, * with yarn at *front* of work insert needle from top to bottom under the 2 horizontal threads in next st in row below, P through these 2 horizontal threads, leave st on left needle, P same st on left needle, drop st from left needle, pass the 2nd st on right needle over first st on right needle **(Purl Twist— PT),** K 1, P 4, K 1, **PT;** * K 6, P 4, K 6; rep between *'s once, K 1.

Row 4: P 1, * **KT,** P 1, **Cable 4,** P 1, **KT;** * P 5, sl next st to dp needle and hold at *back,* K next 2 sts, P then K in front loop of st on dp (1 st inc in pat), sl next 2 sts to dp needle and hold at *front* of work, P next st, K 2 sts from dp, P 5; rep between *'s, once, P 1.

Row 5: K 1, rep between *'s of Row 3 once; K 5, P 2, K 1, with yarn in *front* insert needle from top to bottom under single horizontal thread in next st in row below, P this st and leave on left needle, P same st, drop st from left needle, pass 2nd st over the first st on right needle (single P twist), K 1, P 2, K 5; rep between *'s of Row 3 once, K 1.

Row 6: P 1, rep between *'s of Row 2 once; P 4, sl next st to dp needle and hold at *back,* K next 2 sts, K st from dp, P 1, **KT,** P 1, sl next 2 sts to dp and hold at *front,* K next st, K 2 sts from dp, P 4; rep between *'s of Row 2 once, P 1.

Row 7: K 1, rep between *'s of Row 3 once; K 4, P 2, work single P twist, K 1, **PT,** K 1, work single P twist, P 2, K 4; rep between *'s of Row 3 once, K 1.

Row 8: P 1, rep between *'s of Row 4 once; P 3, sl next st to dp and hold at *back,* K next 2 sts, P st from dp, **(KT,** P 1) twice, **KT,** sl next 2 sts to dp and hold at *front,* P next st, K sts from dp, P 3; rep between *'s of Row 4 once, K 1.

For Tralee shown at right, see instructions page 40.

NOTE: The 9 Border sts (before and after the semi-colons) at each side are now established with cable every 4th row. The following instructions are for center pat only.

Row 9: K 3, P 2, K 1, **(PT,** K 1) 3 times, P 2, K 3.

Row 10: P 2, sl next st to dp and hold at *back,* K next 2 sts, K st from dp, P 1, **(KT,** P 1) 3 times, sl next 2 sts to dp and hold at *front,* K next st, K sts from dp, P 2.

Row 11: K 2, P 2, work single P twist, K 1, **(PT,** K 1) 3 times, work single P twist, P 2, K 2.

Row 12: P 1, sl next st to dp and hold at *back,* K next 2 sts, P st from dp, **(KT,** P 1) 4 times, **KT,** sl next 2 sts to dp and hold at *front,* P next st, K sts from dp, P 1.

Row 13: K 1, P 2, K 1, **(PT,** K 1) 4 times, **PT,** K 1, P 2, K 1.

Row 14: Sl next st to dp and hold at *back,* K next 2 sts, P st from dp, P 1, **(KT,** P 1) 5 times, sl next 2 sts to dp and hold at *front,* P next st, K sts from dp.

Row 15: P 2, K 2, **(PT,** K 1) 5 times, K 1, P 2.

Row 16: Sl next 2 sts to dp and hold at *front,* P next st, K sts from dp, P 1, **(KT,** P 1) 5 times, sl next 2 sts to dp and hold at *back,* K next 2 sts, P st from dp.

Row 17: Rep Row 13.

Row 18: P 1, sl next 2 sts to dp and hold at *front,* P next st, K sts from dp, **(KT,** P 1) 4 times, **KT,** sl next st to dp and hold at *back,* K next 2 sts, P st from dp, P 1.

Row 19: Rep Row 11, working **PT** as required.

Row 20: P 2, sl next 2 sts to dp and hold in *front,* P next st, K sts from dp, (P 1, **KT)** 3 times, P 1, sl next st to dp and hold at *back,* K next 2 sts, P st from dp, P 2.

Row 21: Rep Row 9.

Row 22: P 3, sl next 2 sts to dp and hold at *front,* P next st, K sts from dp, **(KT,** P 1) twice, **KT,** sl next st to dp and hold at *back,* K next 2 sts, P st from dp, P 3.

Row 23: Rep Row 7, working **PT** as required.

Row 24: P 4, sl next 2 sts to dp and hold at *front,* P next st, K sts from dp, P 1, **KT,** P 1, sl next st to dp needle and hold at *back,* K next 2 sts, P st from dp, P 4.

Row 25: Rep Row 5, working **PT** as required.

Row 26: P 5, sl next 2 sts to dp and hold at *front,* P next 2 sts tog (1 st dec in pat), K sts from dp, sl next st to dp and hold at *back,* K next 2 sts, P st from dp, P 5.

Row 27: Rep Row 3.
Rep from Row 2 for Pat and work to approx 68 inches from beg, ending with Pat Row 53. Bind off in pat.

FINISHING: From right side, overcast panels tog.
(continued on page 40)

13. Athlone

Approximate Size: 54 × 66 inches plus fringe

MATERIALS: Knitting Worsted Weight (4-oz.), 14 skeins

NEEDLES: Boye 14-inch No. 8 **OR SIZE TO GIVE GAUGE**
1 dp or cable needle

GAUGE: 5 sts = 1 inch
6 rows = 1 inch

HOOK: Size G

Afghan is worked in 5 panels.

PATTERN 1: Worked on 6 sts.

Row 1: P 1, sl next 2 sts to dp needle and hold at *front*, K next 2 sts, K 2 from dp, P 1.

Row 2: K 1, P 4, K 1.
Rep these 2 rows for Pat 1.

STITCHES FOR PAT 2

LEFT TWIST 3 (LT3): Sl next 2 sts to dp needle and hold at *front* of work, K next st, K 2 sts from dp needle.

RIGHT TWIST 3 (RT 3): Sl next st to dp needle and hold at *back* of work, K next 2 sts, K st from dp needle.

PATTERN 2: Worked on 12 sts.

Row 1: (**LT3**, K 6, **RT3**).

Row 2 and All Even-Numbered Rows: Purl.

Row 3: (K 1, **LT3**, K 4, **RT3**, K 1).

Row 5: (K 2, **LT3**, K 2, **RT3**, K 2).

Row 7: (K 3, **LT3**, **RT3**, K 3).

Row 8: Purl.
Rep these 8 rows for Pat 2.

STITCHES FOR PAT 3

LEFT TWIST (LT): Sk next st, K 1 b in next st and leave on left needle, K the skipped st, drop 2 sts from left needle.

RIGHT TWIST (RT): Sk next st, K next st through *front* loop and leave on left needle, K the skipped st, drop 2 sts from left needle.

PATTERN 3: Worked on 10 sts.

Row 1: K 4, **RT**, K 4.

Row 2 and All Even-Numbered Rows: Purl.

Row 3: K 3, **RT**, **LT**, K 3.

Row 5: K 2, **RT**, K 2, **LT**, K 2.

Row 7: K 1, **RT**, K 4, **LT**, K 1.

Row 9: **RT**, K 4, (turn, P first 2 sts, turn, K same 2 sts) twice, K next 2 sts, **LT**.

Row 11: **LT**, K 6, **RT**.

Row 13: K 1, **LT**, K 4, **RT**, K 1.

Row 15: K 2, **LT**, K 2, **RT**, K 2.

Row 17: K 3, **LT**, **RT**, K3.

Row 18: Purl.
Rep these 18 rows for Pat 3.

STITCHES FOR PAT 4

CABLE 9 FRONT (C9F): Sl next 3 sts to dp needle and hold at *front* of work, K next 3 sts, K 3 sts from dp needle, K 3.

CABLE 9 BACK (C9B): K 3, sl next 3 sts to dp needle and hold at *back* of work, K next 3 sts, K 3 sts from dp needle.

PATTERN 4: Worked on 9 sts.

Row 1: K 9.

Row 2 and All Even-Numbered Rows: Purl.

Row 3: C9F.

Rows 5 and 9: Knit.

Row 7: C9B.

Row 10: Purl.
Rep these 10 rows for Pat 4.

SIDE PANEL AT LEFT: Cast on 62 sts.

Row 1: K 1, work first rows of Pat 1 over 6 sts; Pat 2 over 12; Pat 1 over 6; Pat 3 over 10; Pat 1 over 6, then omit first P 1 and rep Pat 1 over next 5 (keeping 1 P st at each side and 1 P st between these cables on following rows); Pat 4 over 9; Pat 1 over 6, K 1.

Row 2 and All Even-Numbered Rows: K 1, P the purl sts and K the knit sts to last st, K 1.
Keeping pats as established, work to approx 66 inches from beg, ending with Row 18 of Pat 3. Bind off in pats.

SIDE PANEL AT RIGHT: Change position of patterns by beg with *last* st of Row 1 and reading backwards.

PATTERN 5: Worked on 33 sts.

Row 1: Purl.

Row 2 and All Even-Numbered Rows: Knit.

Row 3: P 16, in next st, K 1, P 1, K 1, P 1, K 1 (5 sts in 1 st), turn, K 5, turn, P 5; take yarn to back, sl the 2nd, 3rd, 4th, then 5th st on left needle over first st (**POPCORN STITCH-PS**), P 16.

Row 5: P 14, **PS**, P 3, **PS**, P 14.

Row 7: P 12, (**PS**, P 3) twice, **PS**, P 12.

Row 9: P 10, (**PS**, P 3) 3 times, **PS**, P 10.

Row 11: P 8, (**PS**, P 3) 4 times, **PS**, P 8.

Row 13: Rep Row 9.

Row 15: Rep Row 7.

Row 17: Rep Row 5.

Row 19: Rep Row 3.

Rows 21, 23, and 25: Purl.

Row 27: Rep Row 3.

Row 29: Rep Row 5.

Row 31: P 12, **PS**, P 7, **PS**, P 12.

Row 33: P 10, **PS**, P 11, **PS**, P 10.

Row 35: P 8, **PS**, P 7, **PS**, P 7, **PS**, P 8.

Row 37: Rep Row 33.

Row 39: Rep Row 31.

Row 41: Rep Row 29.

Row 43: Rep Row 27.
K 1 row, (P 1 row, K 1 row) 3 times.
Rep these 50 rows for Pat 5.

SECOND and FOURTH PANEL: Panel is worked using Pat 1 and Pat 5. Cast on 49 sts.

(continued on page 40)

39

14. Tralee

(*Shown at right on page 36*)

Approximate Size: 52 × 68 inches

MATERIALS: Knitting Worsted Weight (4-oz.), 11 skeins

NEEDLES: Size 9 **OR SIZE TO GIVE GAUGE**

1 dp or cable needle

HOOK: Size G

GAUGE: 5 sts = 1 inch
11 rows = 2 inches

Afghan is worked in one piece.

PATTERN 1: Worked on 29 sts.

Row 1 (right side): K 1, * P 1, K 1; rep from * to end.

Row 2: P 1, * K 1, P 1; rep from * to end.

Row 3: P 1, * K 1, P 1; rep from * to end.

Row 4: K 1, * P 1, K 1; rep from * to end.
Rep these 4 rows for Pat 1.

PATTERN 2 (Cable Pat): Worked on 18 sts.

Row 1 (right side): K 1, P 2, K 12, P 2, K 1.

Row 2 and All Even-Numbered Rows: P 1, K 2, P 12, K 2, P 1.

Rows 3 through 6: Rep Rows 1 and 2 twice.

Row 7: K 1, P 2, sl next 3 sts to dp needle, hold at *back* of work, K next 3 sts, K 3 from dp, sl next 3 sts to dp, hold at *front* of work, K next 3 sts, K 3 from dp, P 2, K 1.

Row 8: Rep Row 2.
Rep these 8 rows for Pat 2.

AFGHAN

Cast on 264 stitches.

Row 1: Work first rows of Pat 1 over 29 sts; * Pat 2 over 18 sts; Pat 1 over 29 sts; rep from * 5 times.
Keeping Pats as established work to approx 68 inches from beg, ending with Row 8 of Pat 2. Bind off in pat.

FINISHING: From right side work 1 row sc around afghan, spacing sts to keep edges flat and working 3 sc at corners. Join with a sl st. Ch 1, **do *not* turn.**

Row 2: Sc in each sc, 3 sc in corner sts, join. Ch 1, turn.

Row 3: From wrong side work sl st loosely in each sc. Join, fasten off. Steam lightly.

ATHLONE (*continued from page 39*)

Row 1: K 1, work Pat 1 over 6 sts; K 1, Pat 5 over 33; K 1; Pat 1 over 6; K 1.
Keeping 1 st at each edge in garter st and remaining sts in Pats as established, work to same number of rows as side panels ending with Row 46 of Pat 5. Bind off in pats.

STITCHES FOR PAT 6

CABLE FRONT (CF): Sl next 2 sts to dp and hold at *front*, K next 2 sts, K 2 from dp.

CABLE BACK (CB): Sl next 2 sts to dp and hold at *back*, K next 2 sts, K 2 from dp.

PATTERN 6: Worked on 36 sts.

Row 1: (K 2, **CB**, **CF**, K 2) 3 times.

Row 2 and All Even-Numbered Rows: Purl.

Row 3: (**CB**, K 4, **CF**) 3 times.

Row 5: Knit.

Row 7: (**CF**, K 4, **CB**) 3 times.

Row 9: (K 2, **CF**, **CB**, K 2) 3 times.

Row 11: Knit.

Row 12: Purl.
Rep these 12 rows for Pat 6.

CENTER PANEL: Panel is worked using Pat 1 and Pat 6. Cast on 50 sts.

Row 1: K 1, work Pat 1 over 6 sts; Pat 6 over next 36, Pat 1 over next 6, K 1.
Keeping 1 st at each edge in garter st and remaining sts in pat as established, work to same number of rows as on Side Panel, ending with Row 18 of Pat 6. Bind off in pats.

FINISHING: With wrong side of panels tog, matching rows and picking up 1 loop of sts, overcast panels tog. From right side, work 1 row sc around afghan, spacing sts to keep edges flat and working 3 sc at corners, join and turn. From wrong side, work 1 dc in each sc, working 3 dc at corners.

FRINGE: Wrap yarn around an 8-inch cardboard. Cut at 1 end. Using 6 strands knot fringe in first and every 3rd dc on ends.

KILKENNY (*continued from page 37*)

BORDER — Rnd 1: Join yarn at center of 1 edge, ch 3, sk 1 sp, * 1 sc in next sp, ch 2; rep from * around. Join with a sl st in first ch. Fasten off.

Rnd 2: Join yarn in any sp between sc's, ch 4, 1 dc in *front* of next ch 2, * 1 dc in next sp between sc's, ch 2, 1 dc in *back* of next ch–2; rep from *, join with a sl st, fasten off.

Rnd 3: Join yarn in any sc of first rnd, ch 4, 1 dc in *front* of next sc of first rnd, * ch 2, 1 dc in *back* of next sc of first rnd, ch 2, 1 sc in front of sc of first rnd; rep from *, join with a sl st, fasten off. Steam seams and border.

TASSELS: Lay an 8-inch strand of yarn at top of an 8-inch cardboard. Wrap yarn 20 times around cardboard. Tie strand at top tightly around wrapped yarn. Cut yarn at other end. Wind a strand around tassel 1 inch from top, tie tightly and draw ends into center of tassel. Join to afghan as shown.

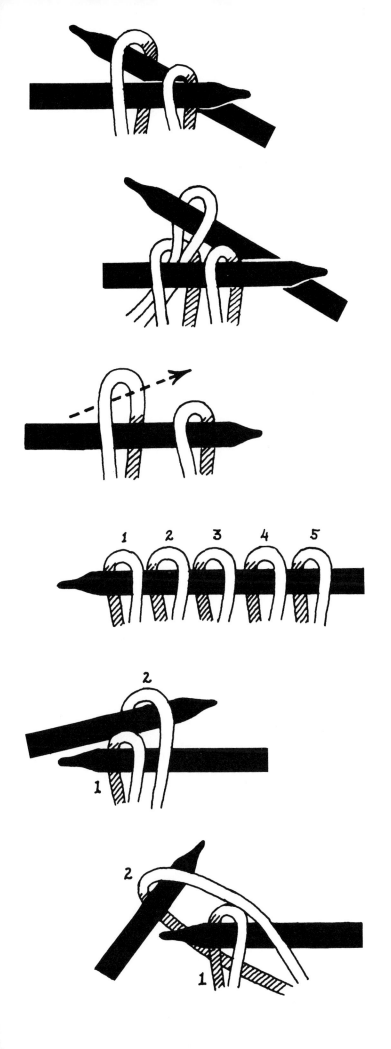

Left Twist

Sk 1 st, K next st through back loop (right needle is kept behind left needle).

Shows st drawn through. Bring right needle back to the front and K the skipped st (through front or back loop as specified in instructions) and drop 2 from left needle. A Left Twist is just the reverse of a Right Twist, slanting toward the left.

Purl Through Back Loop

This is the one that has puzzled many knitters — yet it is quite easy to do. Arrow in diagram shows direction right needle is inserted through stitch. Keep yarn in front of work and just twist your right needle to go through st as shown, bringing point of right needle back to the front and **below** the left needle. Purl the stitch.

POPCORN OR BOBBLE

There are many different ways of working these, but the principle is the same for many. An increase of several sts is made in 1 st (5 in our example) and several rows are worked on just these sts. The extra sts are then passed one at a time (beg with 2nd as shown, then 3rd, 4th and 5th) over the first st and off the needle. One st remains.

41

Section 3.
Special Interest Afghans

The special afghans are collected for the individual who desired a particular design. Although many of these are applicable to certain areas of our country, there are some that have been old favorites for many long years. I hope you will come to enjoy and remake many of these afghans over and over as so many people have.

15.
ABC's Afghan

Approximate Size 51 × 66 inches

MATERIALS: Knitting Worsted Weight, 7 MC and 1 each of 7 other colors

AFGHAN HOOK: 14-inch or Flexible Size H **OR SIZE TO GIVE GAUGE**

CROCHET HOOK: Size G

GAUGE: 4 sts = 1 inch, 3 rows = 1 inch

AFGHAN

Afghan is worked in one piece in basic afghan stitch with worked-in design. With MC chain 190 to measure

approx 48 inches. Work 8 rows basic afghan st. Follow Chart.

FINISHING: Weave in ends.

Border: From right side, with G hook and any CC, work 1 sc in each st and row around entire afghan, with 3 sc in each corner. Join with sl st to first sc, draw MC through lp on hook, break CC.

Rnd 2: Sc in each sc, 3 sc at corners. Join and draw a 2nd CC through lp. Do not break MC.

Rnd 3: Rep Rnd 2, draw MC through, break CC.

Rnd 4: Ch 3, work 1 dc in each sc, 3 dc at corners. Join with sl st to top of ch-3. Fasten off. Steam lightly.

ABC'S

Complete with 9 rows basic afghan st and bind off.

└ Beg with 75th bar on 9th row

16.
The Nantucket Afghan

Approximate Size: 45 × 71 inches

MATERIALS: Knitting Worsted Weight (4-oz.), 8 White (MC), 3 each Light (L), Medium (M) and 2 Dark (D)

NEEDLES: No. 6, **OR SIZE TO GIVE GAUGE**

CROCHET HOOK: Size F

GAUGE: 5 sts = 1 inch
5 ridges = 1 inch

NOTE: Afghan consists of 60 squares (each square should be approximately 6½ inches wide).

LEAF PATTERN: Cast on 3 sts.

Row 1: Yo, K 1, yo, K 1, yo, K 1 (right side).

Row 2: Yo, K 1, P 3, K 2.

Row 3: Yo, K 3, yo, K 1, yo, K 3.

Row 4: Yo, K 2, P 5, K 3.

Row 5: Yo, K 5, yo, K 1, yo, K 5.

Row 6: Yo, K 3, P 7, K 4.

Row 7: Yo, K 7, yo, K 1, yo, K 7.

Row 8: Yo, K 4, P 9, K 5.

Row 9: Yo, K 9, yo, K 1, yo, K 9.

Row 10: Yo, K 5, P 11, K 6.

Row 11: Yo, K 11, yo, K 1, yo, K 11.

Row 12: Yo, K 6, P 13, K 7.

Row 13: Yo, K 13, yo, K 1, yo, K 13.

Row 14: Yo, K 7, P 15, K 8.

Row 15: Yo, K 15, yo, K 1, yo, K 15.

Row 16: Yo, K 8, P 17, K 9.

Row 17: Yo, K 9, sl 1, K 1, psso, K 13, K 2 tog, K 9.

Row 18: Yo, K 9, P 15, K 10.

Row 19: Yo, K 10, sl 1, K 1, psso, K 11, K 2 tog, K 10.

Row 20: Yo, K 10, P 13, K 11.

Row 21: Yo, K 11, sl 1, K 1, psso, K 9, K 2 tog, K 11.

Row 22: Yo, K 11, P 11, K 12.

Row 23: Yo, K 12, sl 1, K 1, psso, K 7, K 2 tog, K 12.

Row 24: Yo, K 12, P 9, K 13.

Row 25: Yo, K 13, sl 1, K 1, psso, K 5, K 2 tog, K 13.

Row 26: Yo, K 13, P 7, K 14.

Row 27: Yo, K 14, sl 1, K 1, psso, K 3, K 2 tog, K 14.

Row 28: Yo, K 14, P 5, K 15.

Row 29: Yo, K 15, sl 1, K 1, psso, K 1, K 2 tog, K 15.

Row 30: Yo, K 15, P 3, K 16.

Row 31: Yo, K 16, sl 1, K 2 tog, psso, K 16.

Row 32: Yo, K across to end of row.

Rows 33 through 38: Repeat Row 32 (41 sts on needle).

Row 39 (right side): Join W and work as follows; *K 2 tog, yo; rep from * across row, ending K 1. 41 sts.

Row 40: P 2 tog, P across row.

Row 41: K 2 tog, K across row.

Row 42: Rep last row.

Row 43: Same as Row 40.

Rows 44 and 45: Same as Row 41.

Row 46: Same as Row 40. 34 sts.

Row 47: * K 2 tog, yo; rep from * across row, ending K 2. 34 sts.

Rep Rows 40 through 46 once. 27 sts.

Rep Row 39 through Row 47.

Rep Row 40 through Row 46.

Rep Row 39 through Row 47.

Rep from Row 40 until 3 sts remain.

NOTE: If you are having a problem after Row 47, here's a suggestion: once you repeat from Row 40 you have the pattern well established, so I would suggest that you just keep going, in pattern, realizing that the ending of the 2 tog, yo rows alternates—and you will easily get down to those 3 stitches without ever having to keep locating the row you are on.

SQUARE: Using No. 6 needles and M, work in Leaf Pattern (this completes one square). Work 23 more squares in same color. Work 24 squares in L and 12 squares in D.

JOINING: Sew tog 4 squares of one shade to form one large square, matching rows and having leaves meet at center (see photograph).

BORDER: Using crochet hook and with right side of work toward you, join M at a corner, ch 3, work 3 dc in corner, work 1 dc, ch 1, 1 dc in each st to corner; rep from * around. Join with a sl st in top of ch-3. Break yarn.

Rnd 2: Join W, ch 3. Work 1 dc in each st and ch of previous rnd. Join with a sl st in top of ch-3.

Rnd 3: Ch 3, work 1 dc in each st. Join with a sl st in top of ch-3.

Rnd 4: Rep Rnd 3. Fasten off.

17.
Indian Head Afghan

Approximate Size: 50 × 64 inches (before fringing)

MATERIALS: Knitting Worsted (4-oz.), 7 MC (Black), 3 CC (White) and 1 each Maroon, Red, Yellow, Aqua, Grey and Beige

AFGHAN HOOK: Size H **OR SIZE TO GIVE GAUGE**

CROCHET HOOK: Size H

GAUGE: 4 sts = 1 inch
7 rows = 2 inches

AFGHAN

Afghan is worked in 3 panels, then embroidered and assembled.

CENTER PANEL: With MC and afghan hook, chain 80 to measure approx 20 inches. Work in basic afghan st for 189 rows. Bind off. Embroider in Cross Stitch following Chart.

SIDE PANELS (Make 2): With MC, chain 41 to measure approx 10 inches. Work in basic afghan stitch, changing colors as follows: * 33 rows MC, ** 1 M (Maroon), 1 CC, 2 MC, 1 CC, 1 M **, 33 CC; rep between **'s once; rep from * once, work 33 MC and bind off. Embroider in Cross Stich following Chart.

FINISHING: Block panels. Use H crochet hook and work from right side of work on long sides of panels.

Center Panel Border (worked on both sides) — **Row 1:** Join M at corner, ch 1 and work 1 sc in each row, ch 1, turn. **Row 2:** Sc in each sc, ending last sc by drawing CC through last 2 lps, ch 1 turn. Work 2 rows sc with CC, drawing MC through last 2 lps of last sc on 2nd row, ch 1, turn. Work 2 rows MC and fasten off.

Side Panel Border: Work same border on *inner* side only of each panel.

To Join Panels: Hold wrong sides tog and with MC, overcast, matching sts.

Outer Border: Work same border around entire afghan, working 3 sc in each corner on *every* rnd. Join each rnd with sl st in first sc, ch 1, do not turn. Complete border with a 3rd rnd of MC. Join and fasten off.

FRINGE: Wrap all colors around a 5-inch cardboard and cut at one end. Use 5 strands for each fringe, beg at corner sc and knotting a fringe in every 2nd sc along ends, using color combinations successively as follows: * (2 MC and 1 each Grey, Red, Yellow); (2 MC and 1 each CC, Aqua, Beige); (2 MC and 1 each CC, Red, Yellow); (2 MC and 1 each Aqua, Grey, Beige); rep from *. Trim evenly.

Chart 1 Side Panel
Worked on all MC squares

COLOR KEY
■ = MC (if on CC square)
    CC (if on MC square)
● = Red
● = Beige
✕ = Yellow
△ = Aqua
/ = Maroon

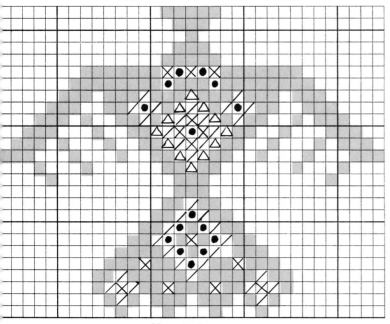

33 center bars
Beg on 5th row of MC square

Chart 2 Side Panel
Worked on all CC squares

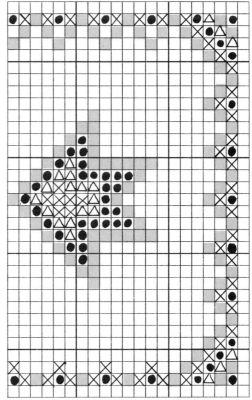

center bar

Worked on 39 bars, beg on 2nd row. Follow chart from right to left to center st, work center st once, then follow chart from left to right.

47

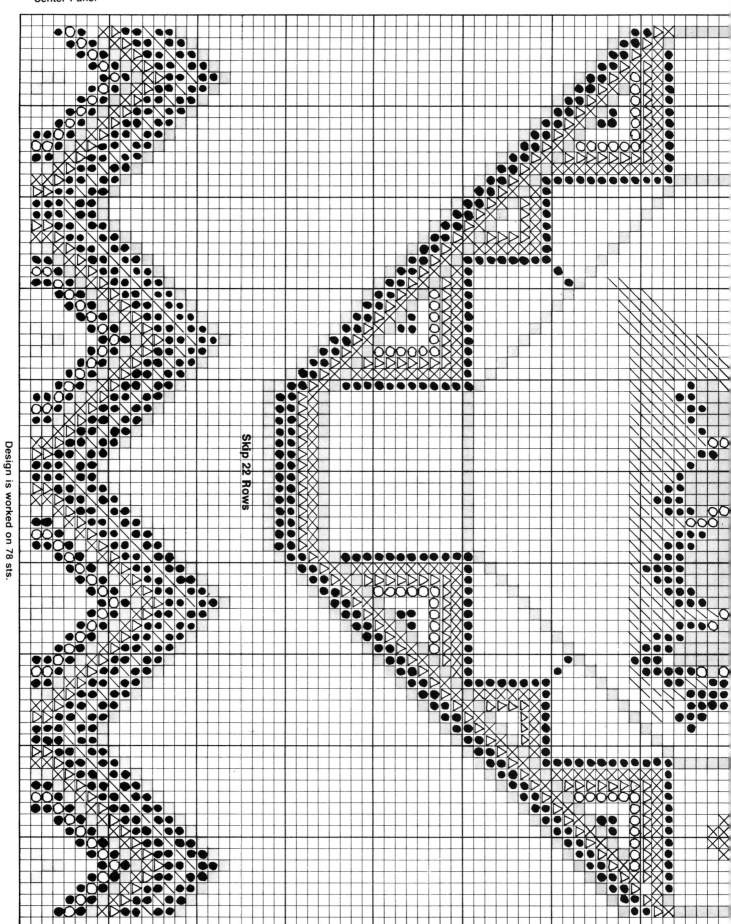

Design is worked on 78 sts.

Skip 22 Rows

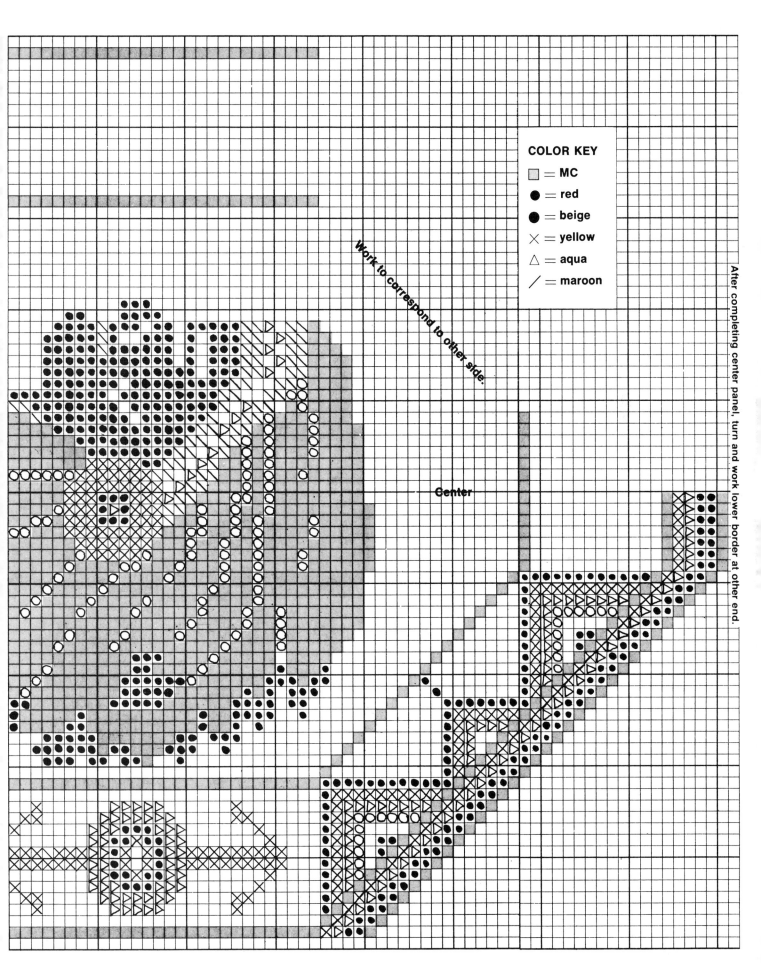

COLOR KEY

☐ = MC
● = red
● = beige
✕ = yellow
△ = aqua
╱ = maroon

Work to correspond to other side.

Center

After completing center panel, turn and work lower border at other end.

18.
Butterfly Afghan

Approximate Size: 51 × 64 inches

MATERIALS: Knitting Worsted Weight (4-oz.), 7 White (MC), 2 each Black and Yellow, 1 each Royal, Lime, Hot Pink

AFGHAN HOOK: 14-inch Size J **OR SIZE TO GIVE GAUGE**

CROCHET HOOK: Size I

GAUGE: 10 sts. = 3 inches
8 rows = 3 inches

PATTERN STITCH: Afghan Stitch with worked-in pattern.

With MC, chain 170 to measure approx 48 inches. Follow Chart for 170 rows. Bind off.

FINISHING: Weave in ends. With MC, from right side, work 1 row sc around afghan, spacing sts to keep edges flat and working 3 sc at each corner. Join with a sl st and fasten off. Block.

FRINGE: Wrap MC around a 10-inch cardboard. Cut at one end. Using 6 strands, knot fringe in first, then every 4th sc along ends. Tie in Double Knot Fringe. Trim evenly.

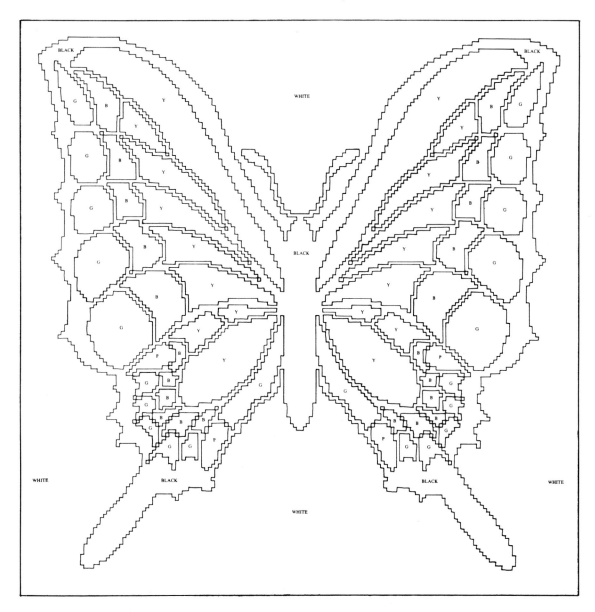

Y = Yellow   P = Hot Pink   B = Royal Blue   G = Lime Green

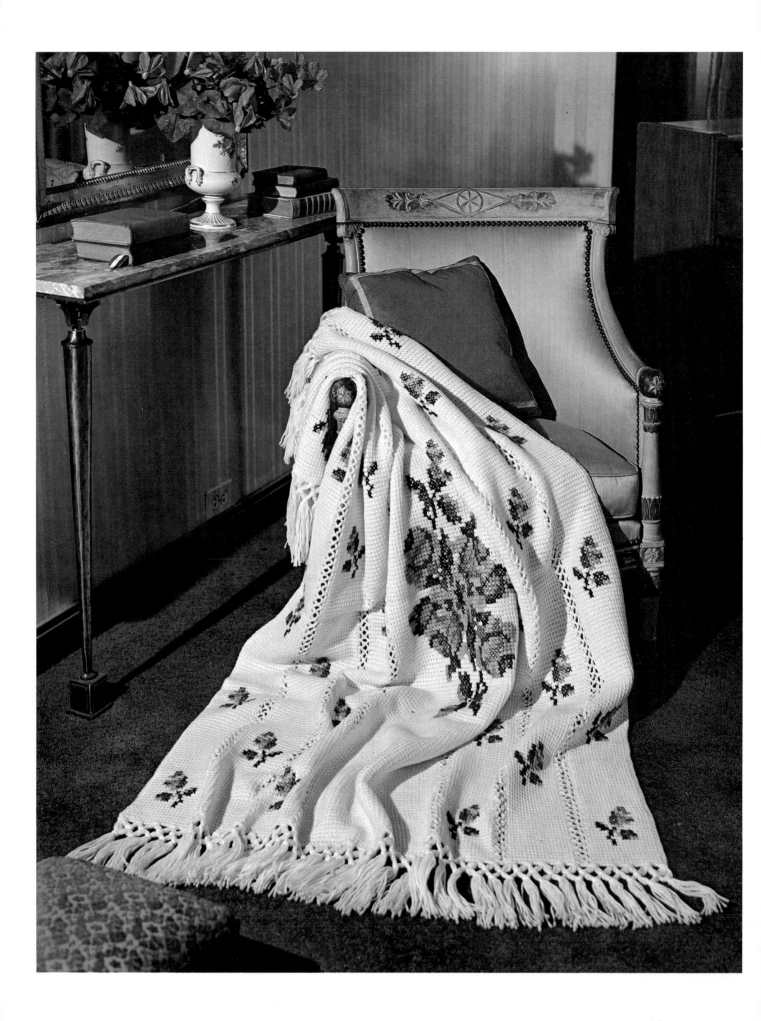

19.
Beguiling Tradition

Approximate Size: 50 × 63 inches

MATERIALS: Knitting Worsted Weight (4-oz.), 10 skeins White (MC); for embroidery 1 skein each of the following colors:

Lt. Rose	Dk. Rose
Rose	Lt. Green
Med. Rose	Green
	Med. Green

Afghan Hook: Size 8 or H **OR SIZE TO GIVE GAUGE**

CROCHET HOOK: Steel 0

Tapestry Needle: 1

GAUGE: 4 sts = 1 inch
3 rows = 1 inch

IMPORTANT: Accurate gauge is absolutely essential.

NOTE: When plain afghan st is worked as a foundation for Cross Stitch Embroidery, avoid drawing loops too high. Work loops off loosely, forming perfect squares on which to embroider.

SIDE PANELS (Make 6): With White and afghan hook ch 20—should measure 5 inches. Work in plain afghan stitch for 190 rows. Bind off. Piece should measure 63 inches.

CENTER PANEL (Make 1): With White and afghan hook ch 56—should measure 14 inches. Work same as side panels. Bind off.

FINISHING: Block each panel.

EMBROIDERY: Cross st is worked over 1 afghan st.

FOR CENTER PANEL: Work large rose design following Chart 1, having first and last row of design on 59th row from each end.

FOR SIDE PANELS: On 1st and 3rd panels work rosebud design A following Chart 2. Begin design A on row 7 and have 5 designs on panels. On 2nd panel follow Chart 3. Begin design on row 26 and have 4 designs on panel. On 5th and 7th panels work rosebud design B following Chart 5. Begin design B on row 7. On 6th panel follow Chart 4. Begin design on row 26.

TO JOIN PANELS: With right side of first panel facing you, using White and Steel crochet hook, work as follows:

Row 1: Work 1 sc in first row, ch 6, skip 1 row, 1 sc in next row, * ch 5, skip 1 row, 1 sc in next row; repeat from *. End ch 5, turn. Join to side of 2nd panel by working 1 sc in first row, * ch 2, 1 sl st in center of last loop on first panel, ch 2, skip 1 row on 2nd panel, 1 sc in next st; repeat from *. End ch 5, 1 sl st in last row of first panel. Fasten off. Join all panels in same way. With White, working from right side, work 1 row sc around afghan, spacing sts to keep edges flat and working 3 sc at corners. Steam afghan.

TRIPLE KNOT FRINGE: Cut White into 20-inch lengths. Use 6 strands for each tassel. Fold 6 strands in half and knot in first st of top edge. Then knot 43 more tassels evenly spaced across top. Divide tassels in half. Knot 2 adjoining halves together about 1½ inches from afghan. Repeat across row. Beginning with free half of first tassel, knot this half with second tassel. Continue to knot 2 adjoining halves together across row. Trim ends evenly.

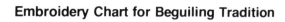

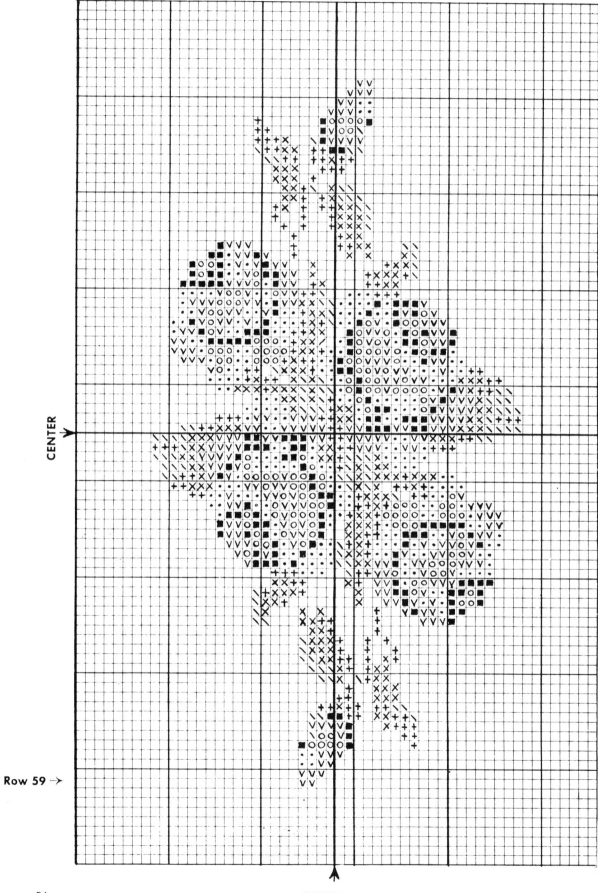

CENTER →

Row 59 →

CENTER ↑

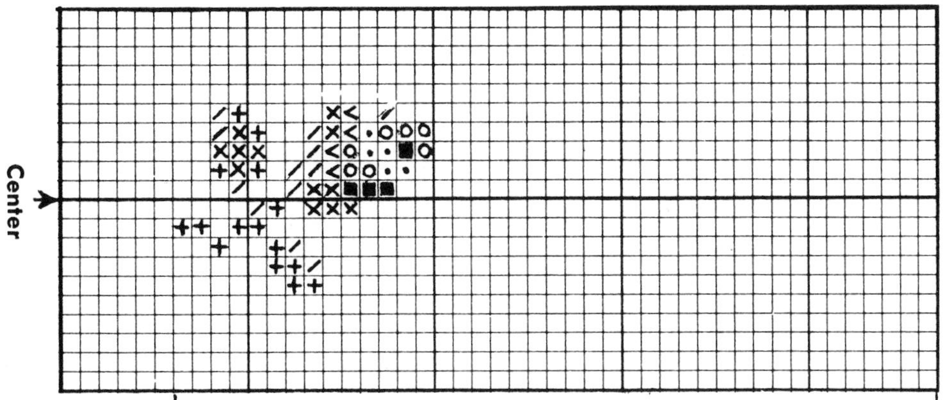

Chart 2—Design A

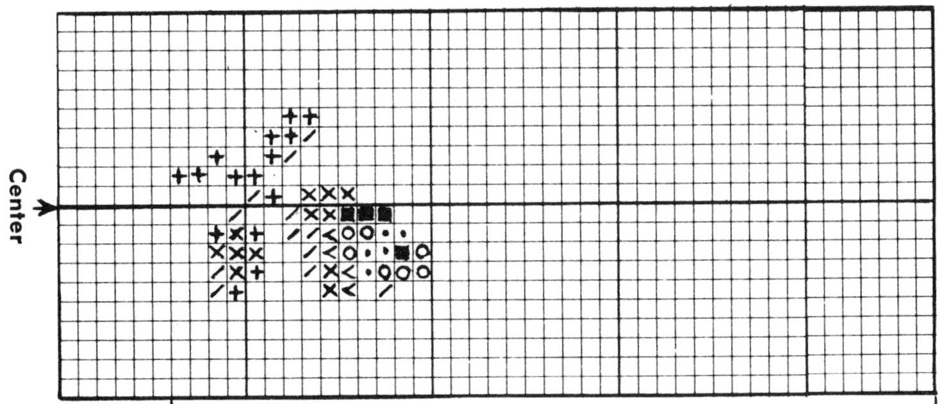

Repeat — 5 ROSEBUDS

Chart 3—Design A

Repeat — 4 ROSEBUDS

COLOR KEY

□	White
●	Lt. Rose
∨	Rose
○	Med. Rose
■	Dk. Rose
╲	Lt. Green
×	Green
+	Med. Green

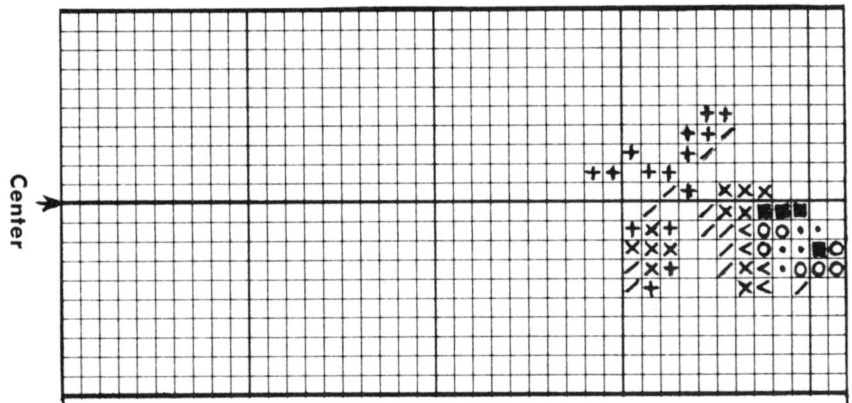

Chart 4—Design B

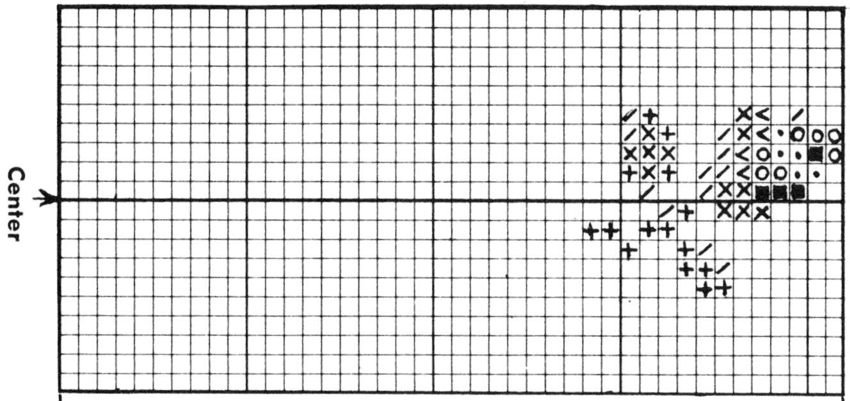

Repeat — 4 ROSEBUDS

Chart 5—Design B

Repeat — 5 ROSEBUDS

55

For instructions for Paul Revere, see page 59.

20.
Independence Hall

Approximate Size: 50 × 60 inches (without border)

MATERIALS: Knitting Worsted Weight (4-oz.), 6 Light Blue (MC), 2 Red and 1 each Dark Red, White, Yellow, Mocha, Dark Brown and Black

AFGHAN HOOK: 14-inch or Flexible Size J **OR SIZE TO GIVE GAUGE**

CROCHET HOOK: Size I

GAUGE: 7 sts = 2 inches
3 rows = 1 inch

AFGHAN

With afghan hook and MC, loosely chain 175. Work in basic afghan st, following the 180 chart rows. Bind off. Weave in ends.

BORDER: Join Mocha at lower left corner. With I hook from right side, sc in each st to corner, 3 sc in corner, sc in each row to top, ch 1, turn. Work sc in each sc, 3 sc in corner st. Fasten off. Join Black at upper right corner and work 2 border rows as before across top and along left side. Fasten off. Join Red in a st not at a corner, ch 2, dc in next sc and in each sc around entire afghan, working 3 dc in each corner st.

21.
Paul Revere

(*Shown on page 57*)

Approximate Size: 50 × 60 inches (without border)

MATERIALS: Knitting Worsted Weight (4-oz.), 3 Red, 5 White, 7 Blue

AFGHAN HOOK: 14-inch or Flexible Size J **OR SIZE TO GIVE GAUGE**

CROCHET HOOK: Size I

GAUGE: 7 sts = 2 inches
3 rows = 1 inch

AFGHAN

With afghan hook and Blue, loosely chain 143, drop Blue, continue chain with 32 Red. First row of chart is worked as follows: Draw up Red lp in 2nd ch from hook and in each of next 30 Red ch, drop Red, pick up Blue from underneath and draw up Blue lp in each of 144 ch. Work off lps (2nd half of basic st) with Blue until 1 Blue st remains, change to Red and work off lps to end. 175 sts in row, 144 Blue, 31 Red. Follow chart, beg with 2nd row until completing the 178 chart rows. Bind off. Weave in ends.

BORDER: Join White at center of bound-off row. With I hook from right side, ch 2, dc in next st and in each st and row around entire afghan, working 3 dc at each corner.
To join rnd, insert hook in top of ch-2, draw Red through. Ch 1, work 1 sc in each dc, 3 sc in corner stitches. Join with sl st to ch-1. Repeat last rnd once, fasten off.

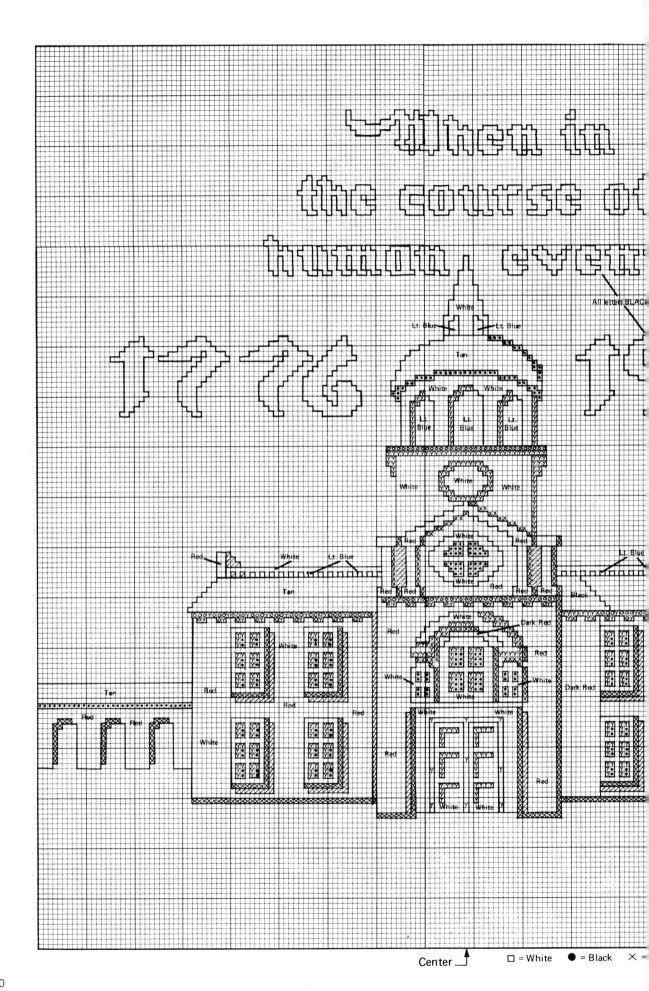

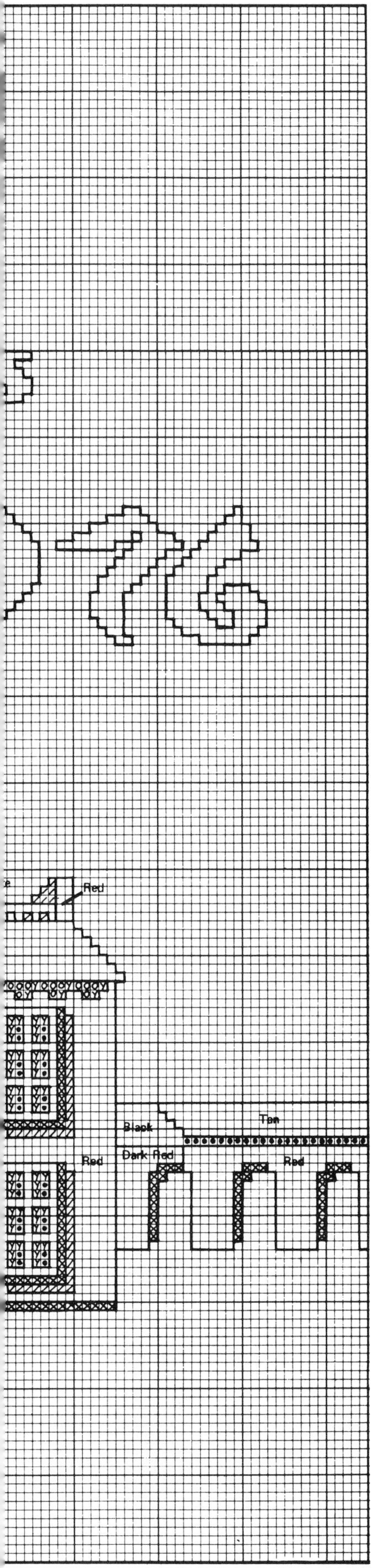

Red

Black   Tan

Red   Dark Red   Red

(Dark)   ╱ = Dark Red   Y = Yellow (Gold)

22.
Zoo Afghan

Approximate Size: 44 × 63 inches (including border)

MATERIALS: Knitting Worsted Weight (4-oz.), 10 skeins White (MC) and 1 each Red, Kelly, Royal Blue, Aqua, Yellow, Orange and Brown

AFGHAN HOOK: Size F **OR SIZE TO GIVE GAUGE**

CROCHET HOOK: Size F

GAUGE: 5 sts = 1 inch
            4 rows = 1 inch

AFGHAN

LARGE BLOCK: With afghan hook, ch 80 to measure approx 16 inches. Work in basic afghan st, working in design from chart.
Complete 60 rows of chart. Bind off.

NARROW BLOCK: With afghan hook, ch 45 to measure approx 9 inches. Work in same manner as large block, following 60 chart rows. Bind off.

FINISHING: Add details, as explained with each chart. Using photograph as guide, assemble blocks in the 3 vertical strips. Hold with wrong sides tog and with crochet hook and MC, sc tog. Then join the strips tog in same way.

BORDER: From right side, with MC and hook, work sc around entire afghan, working 3 sc in each corner. Join with sl st to first sc, ch 1, do not turn. Work 5 more rnds in sc, always working 3 sc in corners. Fasten off.

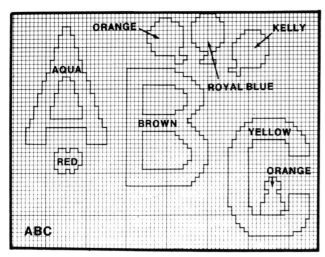

APPLE STEM — kelly ch st.
2 APPLE LEAVES — kelly lazy daisy.
BALLOON STRINGS — royal ch st. Tie bow in royal.
CAT — orange ch st tail, brown french knot eyes, brown straight st whiskers.

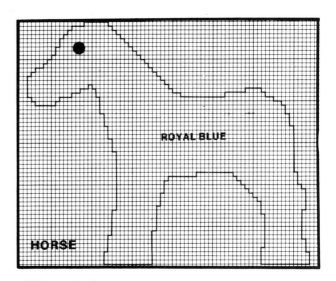

EYE — red satin st.
MANE — 2 rows of 5-inch fringe across top of head and down back of neck to 2 rows before back.
TAIL — 6 5-inch lengths, fringed as tassel.

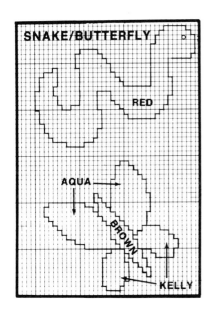

SNAKE — brown french knot for eye, brown ch st for tongue.
BUTTERFLY — brown ch st for feelers, kelly cross st on aqua wings.

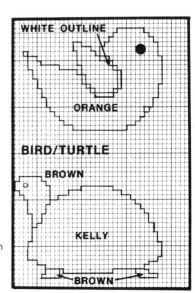

BIRD — eyes, beak and feet in brown ch st. Tail brown straight st.
TURTLE — tail in brown ch st, eye in yellow satin st.

EYES FOR SUN — brown satin st. Mouth brown ch st. Rays ch st.
EYE FOR MOON — brown stem st. line to star, brown ch st.

EYE — yellow ch st.
TAIL — with 4 strands brown, ch 5 inches, leave 1-inch tassel.
EAR — brown, worked same as for hippo.

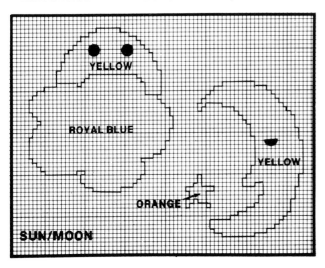

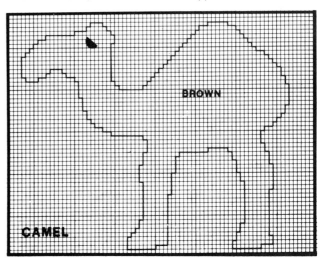

Approximate Size: 36 × 45 inches, without border

MATERIALS: Knitting Worsted Weight (4-oz.), 5 MC and 1 each White (W), Black (B), Aqua (A) and Red (R)

AFGHAN HOOK: 14-inch or Flexible Size H **OR SIZE TO GIVE GAUGE**

CROCHET HOOK: "Boye" Size G

GAUGE: 4 st = 1 inch
3 rows = 1 inch

AFGHAN

Afghan is worked in one piece in basic afghan stitch

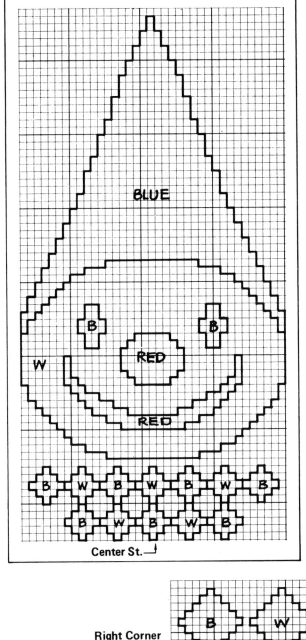

with worked-in design below. With MC, chain 143 to measure 36 inches.
Work 14 rows basic afghan st. Follow Chart.

FINISHING: Weave in ends and block.

NECK RUFF: With right side of afghan toward you and held upside down, join A at right side of face in 5th W row from beg of face. Ch 5, sc in end of W row to left, (ch 5, sc in end of next W row to left) 3 times; ch 5, * sk 1 st, ch 5, sc in next st; rep from * across row, then work other face side to correspond. Ch 3, turn.

Next Row: * Work 8 tr in ch-5 lp, 1 dc in same lp, sc in sc; rep from * to end, fasten off.

HAIR: Wrap R around a 5-inch cardboard and cut at one end. Hold face toward you. Beg at end of same row as top of grin. Fold 2 strands in half, insert hook under strands between W and MC bars, draw fold through, draw cut ends through fold and tighten knot. Knot a fringe in each row around head, ending in corresponding row at opposite side. Knot other fringe between 2 W bars around face as desired, making fringe as thick and shaggy as you like for a happy clown look. Trim as desired. Make a R pompon and sew to top of hat.

BORDER: With G hook and W, from right side work 1 row sc around entire afghan, working 1 sc in each st and in each row and 3 sc at corners. Join with sl st to first sc, fasten off.

Rnd 2: Join A in any sc, ch 3, work 1 dc in each sc, 3 dc in each corner sc. Join to top of ch-3, fasten off.

Rnd 3: Join B to any dc, ch 1, sc in same place with joining and sc in each dc around, with 3 sc at each corner. Join and fasten off. Steam border.

THE HAPPY CLOWN

(1) Beg diamond border on 22nd bar. Work until 11 diamonds.
(2) Work border on both sides.
(3) Beg clown design on 12th row above border.
(4) When 10 diamonds up sides, work top border same as lower border. Complete with 14 rows basic afghan st and bind off.

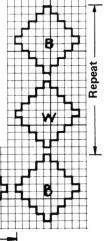

Right Corner Lower Border

|← Repeat →|

24.
Pennsylvania Dutch

Approximate Size: 49 × 63 inches (without fringe)

MATERIALS: Knitting Worsted Weight (4-oz.), 7 Vanilla (MC), 4 Brown, 2 each Peacock, Crimson, Black, 1 each Buttercup, Green

AFGHAN HOOK: 14 inch or Flexible Size H **OR SIZE TO GIVE GAUGE**

GAUGE: 4 sts = 1 inch
3 rows = 1 inch

AFGHAN

Afghan is worked in 1 piece in afghan stitch with worked-in design, see page 11.

With Brown chain 195 to measure 49 inches. On each row of Chart, work to center stitch, omit center st and work back to first st.
Follow Chart on page 70. Bind off.

FINISHING: Sew in ends. Block. If Date and Initials have not been worked in, following Chart work in cross stitch.

FRINGE: Wrap MC around an 8-inch cardboard. Using 4 strands place fringe in every 4th st on end, then tie in double-knot fringe. Fringe other end in same way. Trim evenly.

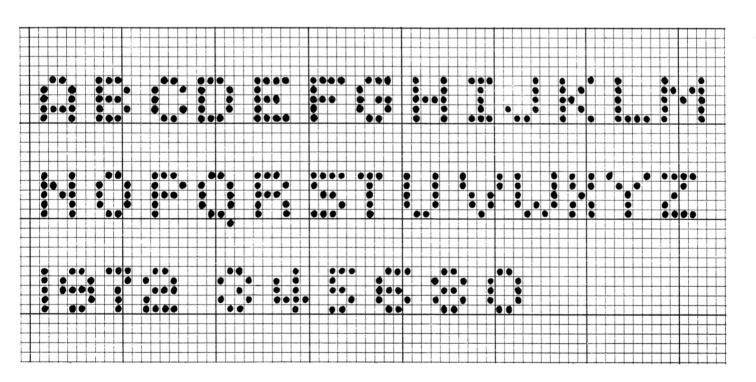

Alphabet Chart

For initials and date if desired

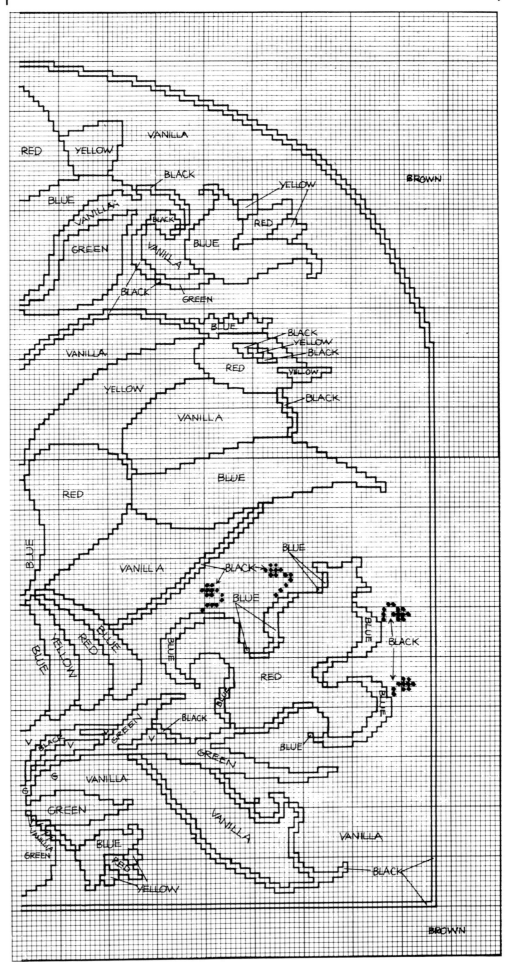

Pennsylvania Dutch Chart

Repeat 97 sts

195 sts across

25.
Chevron Popcorn Afghan

(Shown on bottom right, page 22)

Approximate Size: 53 × 72 inches without fringe

MATERIALS: Knitting Worsted Weight (4-oz.), 14 skeins

AFGHAN HOOK: Size J **OR SIZE TO GIVE GAUGE**

GAUGE: 3 sts = 1 inch
                    3 rows = 1 inch

AFGHAN

PANELS—Make 5: Chain 22. Work 5 rows Basic Afghan St.

Row 6—First Half: Pick up 22 sts.

Row 6—Second Half: Work off 11 lps, ch 3 (picot), work off rem 11 lps.

Row 7—First Half: Pick up 22 sts.

Row 7—Second Half: Work off 10 lps, picot, work off 2 lps, picot, work off rem 10 lps.

Row 8—First Half: Pick up 22 sts.

Row 8—Second Half: Work off 11 lps, picot, work off rem 11 lps. Picots are now est, continue to work picot following chart working next picot on Row 14—Second Half.

Work to end of chart; rep from * to end of chart again; rep from * to **, work 3 rows Basic Afghan St, work Diamond, work 5 rows Basic Afghan St. Bind off, do *not* fasten off.

TO MAKE POPCORN—PO: Work 4 dc in one st, draw up last lp and drop from hook; insert hook in top of first dc, catch dropped lp, draw through dc and tighten.

BORDER: From right side, sc in corner, * work sc in each row along edge (194 sc), ch 1, sc in each st across (22 sc), ch 1, rep from *, join with a sl st to first sc.

Rnd 2: Ch 2 (counts as first dc), dc in next 3 sc, ** * PO, dc in next 5 sc; rep from * to corner end PO, dc in next 3 sc, ch 3, dc in next sc, PO, (dc in next 5 sc, PO) 2 times more, end dc in next 2 sc, ch 3, dc in next 3 sc; rep from ** around ending ch 3, join with a sl st to top of Tch.

Rnd 3: Ch 2 (counts as first dc), dc in next dc, ** * sk 1 dc, dc in next dc, dc in sk dc; rep from * to last 2 sts, dc in last 2 sts, 2 dc in ch-3, ch 2, 2 dc in ch-3 (corner), 2 dc

in first 2 dc, * sk 1 dc, dc in next dc, dc in sk dc; rep from * across to last 2 dc, dc in last 2 dc, corner, rep from ** around, join with a sl st to top of Tch.

Rnd 4: Ch 2 (counts as first dc), through *back* lps, * dc in each dc to corner, dc in ch-2, ch 2, dc in ch-2; rep from * around. Join with a sl st to top of ch-2. Turn.

Rnd 5: From wrong side, sl st in each st and ch around. Fasten off.

TO JOIN PANELS: Join yarn in first st from corner, with wrong sides tog, sc tog top lps of each sl st to end. Fasten off. Join other panels in same way. Block.

FRINGE: Wrap yarn around an 8-inch cardboard and cut at 1 end. Fold 6 strands in half. Insert hook from wrong side in first st on 1 end, draw fold through, draw cut ends through fold. Place fringe in every end st on both ends.

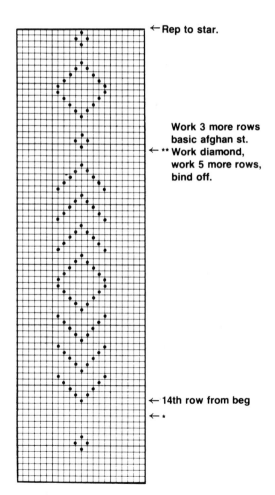

← Rep to star.

Work 3 more rows basic afghan st.
← ** **Work diamond, work 5 more rows, bind off.**

← **14th row from beg**
← *

Section 4.
Traditional Afghans

Knitting and crocheting is the art of creating. And as all these stitches arise from the basic stitches, many of these traditional afghans have grown from there. Whether you are a novice or an expert, you will find many novel and challenging patterns within this collection of afghans.

26.
Granny Crochet Afghan

Approximate Size: 45 × 63 inches

Afghan is 10 squares wide and 14 squares long.

MATERIALS: Knitting Worsted Weight (4-oz.), 5 MC and 1 each of 7 colors

CROCHET HOOK: Size F **OR SIZE TO GIVE GAUGE**

GAUGE: 1 Motif is a 4½ inch square

FINISHED MEASUREMENTS: Approximately 45 by 63 inches.

Each square is made with 4 colors, one round of each, with the last row in the Main Color. The most economical way is to get 7 4-oz. skeins, each in a different color. 4 colors will make approximately 80 squares and the entire afghan takes 140 squares. Then you can mix your colors in any way you desire. You will also need 5 skeins of the Main Color.
Color.

Example, using 4 colors: A, B, C, D, & MC

	1st Square	2nd Square	3rd Square	4th Square
Rnd 1	A	B	C	D
Rnd 2	B	C	D	A
Rnd 3	C	D	A	B
Rnd 4	D	A	B	C
Rnd 5	MC	MC	MC	MC

Alternate all colors in this way.

MOTIF: With A, chain 4. Join with sl st to form a ring.

Rnd 1: Ch 4 (counts as 1 dc, ch 1), 1 dc in ring, * ch 1, 1 dc in ring; rep from * 5 times, ch 1, join with sl st in 3rd ch of ch-4 and fasten off (8 dc in rnd).

Rnd 2: Join B in any ch-1 space, ch 4, 1 dc in same sp, (ch 1, 1 dc in same sp) twice, * ch 1, skip 2 dc, in next ch-1 sp work (1 dc, ch 1, 1 dc) for a V-st, ch 1, V-st in same sp; rep from * twice, ch 1, join with sl st to 3rd ch of ch-4 and fasten off. (There are 4 groups of 2 V-sts).

Rnd 3: Join C in any sp between 2 V-sts of one group. Ch 4, 1 dc in same sp, ch 1, V-st in same sp, * ch 1, V-st in sp between next 2 V-sts, ch 1, (V-st, ch 1, V-st) in sp between next 2 V-sts for corner; rep from *, ending V-st in last sp, ch 1, join with sl st to 3rd ch of ch-4 and fasten off.

Rnd 4: Join D in any corner. Ch 4, 1 dc in same sp, ch 1, V-st in same sp, * (ch 1, V-st in next sp) twice, ch 1, (V-st, ch 1, V-st) in corner sp; rep from *, ending ch 1, join with sl st to 3rd ch of ch-4 and fasten off.

Rnd 5: Join MC in any corner. Ch 4, 1 dc in same sp, ch 1, V-st in same sp, * (ch 1, V-st in next sp) 3 times, ch 1, (V-st, ch 1, V-st) in corner sp; rep from * ending ch 1, join with sl st to 3rd ch of ch-4 and fasten off.
Weave in all ends on wrong side.

FINISHING: Block each motif to a 4½-inch square. The easiest way to arrange your afghan is to lay the motifs out on the floor and then rearrange the colors as you wish.

TO JOIN MOTIFS: Hold with right sides tog and overcast with MC, match sts and working through loops only.

BORDER: Join MC in any corner. Ch 3, 2 dc in same sp, ch 2, 3 dc in same sp (a 3-dc shell), * ch 1, 3 dc in next sp; rep from * to next corner, work 3 dc shell in corner and continue around. Join with sl st to top of ch 3 and fasten off. Weave in ends.

27. Carillon

Approximate Size: 58 × 63 inches

MATERIALS: Knitting Worsted Weight (4-oz.), 6 MC and 1 each B, C, D, E, F

NEEDLES: Circular No. 10 **OR SIZE TO GIVE GAUGE**

CROCHET HOOK: Size H

GAUGE: 4 sts = 1 inch
            5 rows = 1 inch

Afghan is worked vertically in stockinette stitch (K 1 row, P 1 row) following striped pattern given below. Break off color when stripe is complete.

STRIPED PATTERN
30 rows MC;
2 rows B, 8 rows C, 2 rows B, 8 rows D, 2 rows B;
30 rows MC;
2 rows B, 8 rows E, 2 rows B, 8 rows F, 2 rows B (104 rows in Pat).

AFGHAN

Cast on 252 sts for 1 side edge.
Work striped pat until there are 2 complete pats (208 rows).
Work first 82 rows again (290 rows).
Bind off; do **not** break yarn.

FINISHING: Beg from right side, work 3 rows sc along each long side, spacing sts to keep edge flat.
Ch 1 and turn at ends of rows 1 and 2. Fasten off at end of 3rd row.
Along each end, work 2 rows sc.

FRINGE: Fringe matches color stripes of afghans and is tied as follows: 20 in each outer MC panel, 1 in each 2-row stripe, 4 in each 8-row stripe, 15 in other MC stripes. Wrap yarn around a 9-inch cardboard. Cut at one end. Using 2 strands, fringe, **completely covering the 2 rows of sc across ends.** Tie in Triple Knot Fringe.

28. Serenade

Approximate Size: 51 × 73 inches

MATERIALS: Knitting Worsted Weight (4-oz.) 6 MC Blue, 5 White, 1 each of Light Blue and Dark Blue

AFGHAN HOOK: 14 inch Size H **OR SIZE TO GIVE GAUGE**

CROCHET HOOK: Size G

GAUGE: 4 sts = 1 inch
　　　　　 3 rows = 1 inch

ENTIRE AFGHAN IS WORKED IN ONE PIECE IN AFGHAN STITCH.

With Afghan Hook and MC Blue, chain 206 to measure 51 inches. Work 27 rows.

Next Row: With MC pick up 40 loops; join White and pick up 126 loops; join 2nd ball MC and pick up 40 loops to end. Work off loops with matching color.

Repeat chart 2nd row from top and work back to beg.

Continue in this way until there are 165 rows of MC and White. Break White. With MC, work 27 rows. Bind off. Embroider, following charts.

Beg on 7th st from side edges and on 5th row from top and bottom. Place center motif as shown.
With G hook, from right side, work 1 row sc around entire outer edge, working 3 sc in each corner.

Border　　　　　● Lt. Blue　　○ White

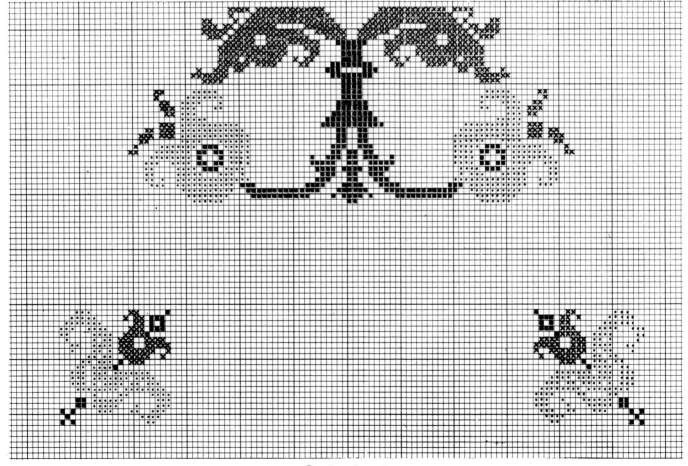

Beg Chart　　　　**Center Panel**　　　　⊠ Lt. Blue　⊠ MC Blue　■ Dk. Blue

29. Forte

Approximate Size: 48 × 66 inches

MATERIALS: Sport Yarn Weight (2-oz.), 7 each A and B, 4 each C and D

NEEDLES: Circular Size 6 **OR SIZE TO GIVE GAUGE**

CROCHET HOOK: Size F

GAUGE: 11 sts = 2 inches
15 rows = 2 inches

With A, cast on 263 sts. Work back and forth. Vertical stripes are added later.

Row 1: K 8, * P 1, (K 2, P 1) twice, K 8, P 1, K 8; rep from * ending K 8.

Row 2: P 8, * K 1, (P 2, K 1) twice, P 8, K 1, P 8; rep from * ending P 8.

Rows 3 and 4: Rep Rows 1 and 2.

Row 5: Rep Row 1. Drop A. Join C.

Rows 6 and 7: With C, rep Rows 2 and 1. Break off C.

Row 8: With A, rep Row 2.

Rows 9 through 12: With A, rep Rows 1 through 4. Drop A. Join D.

Rows 13 and 14: With D, rep Rows 1 and 2. Break off D.

Rows 15 through 26: Rep Rows 1 through 12. Drop A. Join B.

Rows 27 through 38: With B, rep Rows 1 and 2 six times. Drop B. Join D.

Rows 39 and 40: With D, rep Rows 1 and 2. Break off D.

Rows 41 through 52: With B, rep Rows 1 and 2 six times. Break off B. Join A. Rep these 52 rows for pat.

Work pat to approx 66 inches, ending with Pat Row 26. Bind off.

VERTICAL STRIPS: Work from right side, holding CC on wrong side and working a sl st over each P st. Beg with C at first P st, then alternate D and C as in photograph.

FINISHING: Weave in all ends. With right side facing, joint A at cast-on row. Work sc on side edge to first B row, draw B through loop on hook, break A. With B, work sc to next A row, draw A through loop on hook, break B. Continue sc on side of afghan, matching colors. Work opposite side in same way. Block to measurements.

FRINGE: Wrap A, C and D around a 5-inch cardboard. Cut yarn at 1 end. Using 3 strands and beg with C (to match first sl st stripe), single knot fringe, matching colors. Knot 1 fringe at each end of sl st stripes, 1 between sl sts and 4 evenly spaced across 8-st A sections. Trim fringe evenly.

30.
Knitted Ripple Afghan

Approximate Size: 54 × 88 inches fringed

MATERIALS: Knitting Worsted Weight (4-oz.), 12 skeins (1 skein each of 4 shades — very dark, dark, medium, and light) Green (G), Rose (R) and Blue (B)

NEEDLES: No. 9 **OR SIZE TO GIVE GAUGE**

CROCHET HOOK: Size G

GAUGE: 1 pattern (17 sts) = 4½ inches
8 rows = 2 inches

PATTERN STITCH: Work on a multiple of 17 sts plus 4 sts.

Row 1 (right side): K 2, * K 2 tog, K 6, yo (an inc), K 1 and mark this st, yo (another inc), K 6, sl 1 as to K, K 1, psso; rep from *, ending K 2.

Row 2: K 2, P to last 2 sts, working yo's as sts, K 2. Rep these 2 rows for pat.

AFGHAN

With Darkest G cast on 208 sts.

Work pat as follows:* 2 rows darkest G
2 rows dark G
2 rows medium G
2 rows light G

Rep these 8 rows with B, then with R. Rep from * 10 times. Work 8 rows G.

Bind off loosely with G.

FRINGE: Wrap darkest G loosely 48 times around a 10-inch cardboard. Cut at 1 end. This makes 20-inch strands. Fold 8 strands in half, insert crochet hook from wrong side in first cast-on st, catch folds with hook and draw through, then draw cut ends through fold. Tighten to form knot on right side. Wrap all other colors 32 times around cardboard and cut.

Following color sequence as on afghan, place fringe at each point and at space between decs on cast-on and bound-off edges. Trim fringe evenly.

31. Galaxy

Approximate Size: 50 × 60 inches

MATERIALS: Sport Yarn Weight (2-oz.), 1 each of 10 colors, 1 for outer edging and 5 yds of a color for each center flower

NOTE: If you would like to use fewer colors, one 2-oz. skein will make 12 borders plus 10 flowers or approx 46 flowers.

HOOK: Size G **OR SIZE TO GIVE GAUGE**

GAUGE: 1 motif = 5 inches square

AFGHAN

MOTIF: Use desired colors for flowers and make 12 motifs with the same color borders. Rep with other 9 colors. 120 motifs in all. With a flower color ch 5. Join with a sl st to form a ring.

Rnd 1: Ch 1, 18 sc in ring. Join with a sl st to first sc.

Rnd 2: Ch 3, yo hook twice, insert hook in same st with ch-3, draw yarn through, (yo and through 2 lps) twice, (leaving 2 lps on hook, for an unfinished tr-UTR); work UTR in each of next 2 sts, yo and through 4 lps, ch 3, sc in same sc with last UTR, * ch 3, UTR in each of next 3 sts, yo and through 4 lps, ch 3, sc in same sc with last UTR (petal); rep from * 4 times, join with a sl st to same st as first ch-3. 6 petals. Break yarn.

Rnd 3: Join border color to top of a petal, sc in same place with joining, * ch 6, sc in top of next petal; rep from * ending ch 6, sl st in first sc, ch 1.

Rnd 4: Sc in first sc, * 11 sc in next ch-6 lp, 10 sc in next ch-6 lp; rep from * twice, join to first sc. 64 sc.

Rnd 5: Ch 4 and count as dc, ch 1, (sk next st, dc in next st, ch 1) 3 times, * sk next st, in next st work dc, ch 1, dc for corner, (ch 1, sk next st, dc in next st) 7 times, ch 1; rep from *, ending (ch 1, sk next st, dc in next st) 3 times, ch 1, join to 3rd ch of ch-4.

Rnd 6: Ch 4, (dc in next dc, ch 1) 3 times; in corner ch-1 sp work (dc, ch 1) 3 times, * sk next dc; (dc in next dc, ch 1) 7 times, work corner, rep from *, ending (dc in next dc, ch 1) 3 times, join and fasten off.

FINISHING: Assemble motifs in 10 strips of 12 matching border colors. Hold 2 motifs with wrong sides tog and overcast, matching dc to dc and ch to ch. Join strips tog in same way, in desired color sequence.

BORDER: With desired color, from right side, work 1 row sc around afghan, spacing sts to keep edge flat and working 3 sc at corners, join, *do not* turn. Working from left to right, work sc in each sc, 3 sc at corners, (backward crochet). Join and fasten off. Steam afghan, do *not* press flowers flat.

32.
Allegro

(Shown on opposite page at right)

Approximate Size: 50 × 61 inches

MATERIALS: Knitting Worsted Weight (4-oz), 12 skeins

NEEDLES: Circular No. 9 **OR SIZE TO GIVE GAUGE**

CROCHET HOOK: Size F

GAUGE: 9 sts = 2 inches
5 rows = 1 inch

PATTERN STITCH: Worked on a multiple of 22 sts plus 5. Slip the sl sts as to P with yarn at **back** of work. Be sure to keep Popcorns pulled to **right** side of work.

Row 1 and All Odd-Numbered Rows: K 2, P to last 2 sts, K 2.

Row 2 (right side): K 2, sl 1, K 1, psso, * K 1, yo, K 1, yo, K 6, sl 1, K 2 tog, psso the 2 tog, K 6, yo, K 1, yo, K 1, sl 1, K 2 tog, psso; rep from * to last 4 sts, K 2 tog, K 2.

Row 4: K 2, sl 1, K 1, psso, * K 2, yo, K 1, yo, K 5, sl 1, K 2 tog, psso, K 5, yo, K 1, yo, K 2, sl 1, K 2 tog, psso; rep from * to last 4 sts, K 2 tog, K 2.

Row 6: K 2, sl 1, K 1, psso, * K 2; in next st, drawing loops up slightly, K in front, back, front, back, front (5 loops), insert point of left needle in 2nd loop on right needle and pass over first loop, pass 3rd, 4th and 5th loop over first in same way (popcorn); yo, K 1, yo, K 4, sl 1, K 2 tog, psso, K 4, yo, K 1, yo, popcorn, K 2, sl 1, K 2 tog, psso; rep from * to last 4 sts, K 2 tog, K 2.

Row 8: K 2, sl 1, K 1, psso, * K 3; popcorn, yo, K 1, yo, K 3, sl 1, K 2 tog, psso, K 3, yo, K 1, yo, popcorn, K 3, sl 1, K 2

tog, psso; rep from *, to last 4 sts, K 2 tog, K 2.

Row 10: K 2, sl 1, K 1, psso, * K 4, popcorn, yo, K 1, yo, K 2, sl 1, K 2 tog, psso, K 2, yo, K 1, yo, popcorn, K 4, sl 1, K 2 tog, psso; rep from *, to last 4 sts, K 2 tog, K 2.

Row 12: K 2, sl 1, K 1, psso, * K 5, popcorn, yo, K 1, yo, K 1, sl 1, K 2 tog, psso, K 1, yo, K 1, yo, popcorn, K 5, sl 1, K 2 tog, psso; rep from * to last 4 sts, K 2 tog, K 2.

Row 14: K 2, sl 1, K 1, psso, * K 6, popcorn, yo, K 1, yo, sl 1, K 2 tog, psso, yo, K 1, yo, popcorn, K 6, sl 1, K 2 tog, psso; rep from * to last 4 sts, K 2 tog, K 2.

Rep these 14 rows for pat.

AFGHAN

Cast on 225 sts. Work back and forth in pat until there are 22 pats of 14 rows each, or to desired length. Bind off in pat.

FINISHING: From right side, work 1 row sc on all edges, spacing sts to keep edges flat and working 3 sc at each corner. Join with a sl st. Ch 1, turn. Work 1 sc in each sc on side edges, 3 sc at corners, AND, on ends, work 1 sc in first sc, * ch 3 skip 2 sc, 1 sc in next sc; rep from * across and end with 1 sc in last sc.

Block to measurements.

FRINGE: Wrap yarn around a 12-inch cardboard. Cut yarn at 1 end. Using 8 strands knot fringe under first and every 2nd ch-3 loop. Tie for Triple Knot Fringe. Trim evenly.

33.
Legato

(Shown on opposite page at left)

Approximate Size: 51 × 61 inches

MATERIALS: Knitting Worsted Weight (4-oz.), 8 MC and 3 CC

CROCHET HOOK: Size G **OR SIZE TO GIVE GAUGE**

GAUGE: 1 shell = 2 inches
10 shell rows = 7 inches

SHELL STRIP (Make 8): With CC, ch 4, join with a sl st to form ring.

ROW 1: Ch 3, turn, 3 dc in ring, ch 2, 4 dc in ring, ch 3, turn.

Row 2: 3 dc in ch-2 sp, ch 2, 3 dc in same ch-2 sp, dc in top of turning ch-3. Ch 3, turn. Rep Row 2 until there are 80 shell rows. Fasten off.

DOUBLE CROCHET EDGE (work on both sides of 6 of the shell strips).

Row 1 (right side): Join MC at top of first ch-3 of **first** shell row, ch 2, work 2 dc in first sp at side, * 3 dc in next sp; rep from * to last sp, work 2 dc in last sp, dc in next dc. Ch 1, turn.

Row 2: Working through **top** loop only and taking care not to draw work tightly, sl st in each dc, ending with dc in top of ch-3. Ch 3, turn.

Row 3: Skip first sl st; working through **top** loop only, dc in each sl st. Ch 1, turn.

Rows 4 and 5: Rep Rows 2 and 3.
(Continued on page 87)

34. Elegant

Approximate Size: 41 × 51 inches

MATERIALS: Sport Yarn Weight (2-oz.), 10 skeins

HOOK: Size F **OR SIZE TO GIVE GAUGE**

GAUGE: 1 motif = 5 inches square

AFGHAN

MOTIF (Make 63): Ch 8, join with a sl st to form a ring.

Rnd 1: Ch 3, (counts as 1 dc), 15 dc in ring, join with a sl st to top of ch-3.

Rnd 2: Ch 4, (counts as dc and ch-1) * dc in next dc, ch 1; rep from * around, ending sl st in 3rd ch of ch-4.

Rnd 3: Ch 3, 2 dc in next ch-1 sp, * dc in next dc, 2 dc in next ch-1 sp; rep from * around, ending sl st in top of ch 3. 48 dc.

Rnd 4: * Ch 5 sk 2 dc, sc in next dc, (ch 3, sk 2 dc, sc in next dc) 3 times, rep from * 3 times, ending last rep ch 3, sk 2 dc, sc in same place with sl st of last rnd, sl st under ch-5 lp.

Rnd 5: Ch 3, 2 dc in first ch-5 lp, ch 2, 3 dc in same lp (corner shell), ch 1, (3 dc in next ch-3 lp, ch 1) 3 times, * in next ch-5 lp work 3 dc, ch 2, 3 dc, ch 1, (3 dc in next ch-3 lp, ch 1) 3 times, rep from * twice, join with a sl st to top of ch-3.

Rnd 6: Sl st in each st to ch-2 of first corner, sl st under ch-2, ch 3, 2 dc in same ch-2 sp, ch 2, 3 dc in same sp, ch 1, (3 dc in next ch-1 sp, ch 1) 4 times;* work corner, ch 1, (3 dc in next ch-1 sp, ch 1) 4 times; rep from *

around. Join to top of ch-3. Fasten off.

FINISHING: Hold motifs with right sides tog. Taking up top lps only and matching st for st, (25 sts along each side, counting each dc, chs between shells and 1 ch at each corner), overcast motifs tog in strips of 9 in length and 7 in width.

BORDER—Rnd 1: From right side, join yarn in a ch-2 corner. Ch 1, sc in same sp, ch 1, * (sc in each of next 3 dc, sc in ch-1) 6 times (last sc is in one ch at corner of first motif and there are 24 sc along edge); rep from * on edge of next and each following motif, ending last motif on this side with 1 sc in each of last 3 dc (23 sc on edge of last motif); ch 1, sc under corner ch, ch 1; rep from * along other edges, working next 2 corners as first corner, ending rnd with sc in each of last 3 dc, ch 1, join with sl st to first sc. Do not turn.

Rnd 2: Ch 1, sc in same sc, * ch 3, sk 2 sc, sc in next sc; ch 2, sk 1 sc, sc in next sc; ch 3, sk 2 sc, sc in next sc; rep from * to corner, ending side with ch 3, sk 2 sc, sc in corner sc; working corners to correspond and ending rnd ch 3, sk 2 sc, sl st in first sc of rnd.

Rnd 3: Ch 1, sc in same sc, ch 3, in ch-2 sp work (2 dc, ch 2, 2 dc) shell, ch 3, sk sc after shell, sc in next sc, * ch 3, shell in next ch-2 sp, ch 3, sk sc after shell, sc in next sc; rep from * around, ending ch 3, join with sl st to first sc.

Rnds 4 and 5: Ch 1, sc in same sc, * ch 3, shell in ch-2 sp of next shell, ch 3, sc in next sc; rep from * around, ending ch-3, sl st in first sc of rnd.

Rnd 6: Ch 1, sc in same sc, * ch 5, 5 dc in ch-2 sp of shell, ch 5, sc in next sc; rep from * around, ending ch 5, join with sl st to first sc and fasten off.

Legato (*continued from page 85*)

Row 6: Rep Row 2. Fasten off.

Join MC on opposite side of shell strip, at **last** shell row. Work 6 rows as on other side.

DOUBLE CROCHET EDGE (work on **one side only** of remaining 2 shell strips). On 1 strip, begin at first shell row and work 6 rows as before.

On 2nd strip, begin at **last** shell row and work as before. Block panels.

TO JOIN PANELS: With right sides of 2 panels tog and with first row of shell sts at lower edge, overcast the 6 panels tog through top loop of each st from each panel. At each side, join MC edge of remaining 2 panels. (CC shell at each outer edge.)

BORDER: Join MC under ch-3 of first shell row at outer edge. Ch 3 and work from right side.

Row 1: Work 2 dc in same sp with joining, * 3 dc in next

sp; rep from * to last sp on edge, (3 dc, ch 2, 3 dc) in last sp for corner; ch 1, sc in first ch-2 of shell, ch 1, 2 dc under end st of dc row, dc in sl st row; rep from * to joining row, dc in joining; continue in this way on all sides, ending ch 2, 3 dc in same sp as 2 dc at beg of row. Join with sl st to top of ch-3. Ch 1, turn.

Row 2: Working through **top** loop only, sl st in each st and work 3 sc in ch-2 at each of 4 corners, join. Ch 3, turn.

Row 3: Working through **top** loop, dc in each st, (2 dc, ch 2, 2 dc) in center st at corners, join. Ch 1, turn.

Rows 4 and 6: Same as Row 2. Fasten off at end of Row 6.

Row 5: Same as Row 3.

FRINGE: Wrap MC around a 7-inch cardboard. Cut at one end. Using 2 strands, single knot fringe in corner, then in every 2nd sl st across ends of afghan. Trim evenly.

35. Ballade

Approximate Size: 54 × 68 inches

MATERIALS: Knitting Worsted Weight (4-oz.), 8 MC and 2 each A and B

CROCHET HOOK: Size I **OR SIZE TO GIVE GAUGE**

GAUGE: 1 shell (5 dc) and 1 sc = 2 inches
10 rows = 5 inches

AFGHAN

With MC, ch 164 to measure approx 54½ inches.

Row 1: Sc in 2nd ch from hook and each ch to end (163 sc). Ch 1, turn.

Row 2: Sc in first sc, * skip 2 sc, 5 dc in next sc (shell), sk 2 sc, sc in next sc; rep from * to end (27 shells). Ch 3, turn.

Row 3: 2 dc in first sc (half shell with ch-3 counting as 1 dc), * sc in center dc of next shell, shell in next sc; rep from *, ending last rep half shell (3 dc) in last sc. Ch 1, turn.

Row 4: Sc in first dc, * shell in next sc, sc in center dc of next shell; rep from *, ending last rep sc in last dc. Ch 3, turn.

Row 5: Rep Row 3. Break MC, draw A through loop on hook. Ch 1, turn.

Row 6: With A, rep Row 4, omitting ch-3 at end of row. Drop A, draw B through loop on hook, turn.

Row 7: Insert hook in first dc of Row 5, yo and draw loop through dc and loop on hook, ch 3, 2 dc in same dc, sc in center dc of next shell of row 6; * working over next sc of Row 6, work shell in center of shell of Row 5; sc in center dc of next shell of Row 6; rep from *, ending last rep half shell in last dc of Row 5. Break B, draw MC through loop. Ch 1, turn.

Row 8: Sc in first dc, * shell in center dc of shell of Row 6, sc in center of dc of shell of Row 7; rep from *, ending last rep sc in top of turning ch-3. Break MC, draw B through loop.

Row 9: Work same as Row 7, inserting hook in first dc of Row 7, working shells in center dc of shells 2 rows below, ending half shell in last dc of half shell. Break B, draw A through loop. Ch 1, turn.

Row 10: Sc in first dc, * shell in center of shell 2 rows below, sc in center of shell of previous row; rep from *, ending last rep sc in top of turning ch-3. Break A, draw MC through loop, turn.

Row 11: Insert hook in top of turning ch of Row 9, yo, draw loop through as before, ch 3, 2 dc in same st, * sc in center of next shell, shell in center of next shell 2 rows below; rep from *, ending last rep half shell in last dc 2 rows below. Ch 1, turn.

Rows 12 and 14: Rep Row 4.

Row 13: Rep Row 3.

Row 15: Rep Row 5.

Rep Rows 6 through 15 until piece measures approx 68 inches, ending with Pat Row 14. Ch 1, turn.

Last row: Hdc in first sc, * hdc in next dc, sc in each of next 3 dc, hdc in next dc, dc in next sc; rep from * to end. Fasten off.

FINISHING: Weave in all ends neatly. Block lightly to measurements.

TASSELS: Wind MC 10 times around a 3-inch cardboard. Cut 1 end. Fold strands in half. Wind another strand tightly several times around folded end (about ½ inch below fold) and tie securely.

With right side facing, insert hook in first st on short end and join MC, * ch 6, slip hook through folded loops of tassel, ch 6, skip 4 sts, sc in next st; rep from * across end. Join tassels on other end in same way.

36.
Libretto

Approximate Size: 49 × 61 inches

MATERIALS: Knitting Worsted Weight (4-oz.), 6 MC and 2 each A, B, and C

CROCHET HOOK: Size J **OR SIZE TO GIVE GAUGE**

GAUGE: 1 Motif = 6 inch square

MOTIF: Worked with 2 colors.
With A, ch 4. Join with a sl st to form a ring.

Rnd 1: Ch 3 (counts as 1 dc), work 15 dc in ring, join with a sl st to top of ch-3. 16 dc.

Rnd 2: Ch 4, * dc in next dc, ch 1; rep from *, ending sl st in 3rd ch of ch-4 (16 ch-1 sps). Break A, draw MC through loop on hook.

Rnd 3: Ch 3, 4 dc in first sp, draw up loop on hook and remove hook (leaving loop free), insert hook from front to back through top of ch-3 and through free loop, drawing loop to hook size, yo and through loops on hook (popcorn), ch 2, * work 5 dc in next sp, draw up loop, remove hook, insert hook in top of first dc and free loop, complete as before, ch 2; rep from * around; join with a sl st to top of ch-3 of first popcorn. Break off MC, draw A through loop on hook.

Rnd 4: Ch 3, 2 dc in last ch-2 sp of last row (3-dc shell), * (3 dc in next ch-2 sp) 3 times; in next sp, work shell, ch 2 and shell (corner); rep from *, ending shell in same sp as first shell, ch 2, join with a sl st to top of ch-3. Break off A, draw MC through loop on hook.

Rnd 5: Through **back** loops, work 1 sc in same st with sl st and in each dc, 3 sc under each ch-2 at corners. Join and fasten off.

Work 20 squares more of A and MC.
Work 21 squares each B and MC, C and MC.

FINISHING: Weave in ends. Block all squares lightly to exact measurement.
Follow diagram for assembling squares.
With right sides of squares tog and using MC, overcast edges tog through top loops of sts.

Border — Rnd 1: Join MC through **back** loop of center sc of a corner. From right side, work 2 sc in same place with joining: * through **back** loops, work 1 sc in each sc to center sc of next corner, work 3 sc under ch-2 at corner; rep from * around, sc in same place as first 2 sc, join with a sl st to first sc. Drop MC, draw A through loop on hook.

Rnd 2: Ch 3, 2 dc in st with joining, * skip 2 sc, 3 dc in next sc (shell); rep from * to 2 sts before center st of corner; in corner st, work shell, ch 2, shell; continue in this way around, ending shell, ch 2, in same st with first shell, join with a sl st to top of ch 3. Break off A, draw MC through loop on hook.

Rnd 3: Through **back** loops, work sc in each st, 3 sc under ch-2 at corners. Join.

Rnd 4: Through **back** loops, work sc in each sc, 3 sc in center st of each corner, join.

Rnd 5: With B, rep Rnd 2.

Rnds 6 and 7: With MC, rep Rnds 3 and 4.

Rnd 8: With C, rep Rnd 2.

Rnds 9 and 10: With MC, rep Rnds 3 and 4.

Fasten off.
Steam afghan lightly to measurements.

Repeat 3 times	A	C	B	A	C	B	A
	B	A	C	B	A	C	B
	C	B	A	C	B	A	C

37. Cadence

Approximate Size: 59 × 68 inches

MATERIALS: Sport Yarn Weight (2-oz.), 16A, 10B, 6C

NEEDLES: No. 10 **OR SIZE TO GIVE GAUGE**

GAUGE: 5 sts = 1 inch
          6 rows = 1 inch

Afghan is worked with double yarn (2 strands held tog).

PATTERN STITCH: Worked on a multiple of 3 sts.

Row 1 (right side): K 1, * skip 2 sts, insert right needle in next st as to P, draw this st over the 2 skipped sts and retain on right needle, K first, then 2nd skipped st *, rep between *'s, ending K 2.

Row 2 and All Even-Numbered Rows: Purl.

Row 3: K 2; rep between *'s of Row 1, ending K 1.

Row 5: Rep between *'s of Row 1.

Row 6: Purl.

Rep these 6 rows for pat.

THREE-COLOR STRIPS (Make 3): With A, cast on 63 sts. P 1 row. Work pat of 2 rows A, 2 rows B, 2 rows C (carry colors not in use loosely along edge of work) to approx 68 inches from beg, or desired length, ending with 2 rows A. Bind off.

ONE-COLOR STRIPS (Make 2 A and 2 B): Cast on 24 sts. Work pat to same number of rows as 3-color strips. Bind off.

FINISHING: With double strand A from right side, work sc on edges of all strips, spacing sts to keep edges flat, **taking care to have same number of sc on sides of all strips,** and working 3 sc at each corner. Join with a sl st. Fasten off.

TO JOIN STRIPS: Use double strand A for joining all strips. Hold an A strip and a 3-color strip with wrong sides tog, insert crochet hook in back loops of first sc at top of both strips, work a sl st loosely; continue in this way in each pair of sc to lower edge. Fasten off. Join C strip to other side of 3-color strip, then join 3-color strip, 2nd C strip, 3-color strip, and 2nd A strip. Block to measurements.

FRINGE: Wrap A around a 9-inch cardboard. Cut at one end. Using 6 strands, fringe in first sc, then in every 2nd sc. Tie for Double Knot Fringe. Trim fringe evenly.

38.
Stadium

Approximate Size: 53 × 78 inches

MATERIALS: Knitting Worsted Weight (4-oz.), 9 MC, 3 each A and B, 2 C

AFGHAN HOOK: Size I **OR SIZE TO GIVE GAUGE**

CROCHET HOOK: Size F

GAUGE: 7 sts = 2 inches
5 rows = 2 inches
MOTIF (with border) = 9 inches square

AFGHAN

MOTIF (Make 39): With afghan hook and MC ch 26 to measure 7 inches.

Row 1—First Half: Sk first ch from hook, * insert hook through top lp only of next ch, yo and draw yarn through ch, forming lp on hook, retain lp on hook; rep from * across ch. There will be same number of lps on hook as number of chs.

Row 1—Second Half: Yo hook and draw through first lp, * yo and draw through 2 lps; rep from * across row until there is 1 lp on hook. This lp is first st of next row.

Row 2—First Half: Sk the first 2 vertical bars (upright sts), insert hook in 3rd vertical bar and draw up lp, retain lp on hook, draw up lp in 2nd (skipped) bar, retain lp on hook (cross st), * sk next bar, draw a lp in next bar, draw lp in sk bar; rep from * to last bar, insert hook under 2 sts forming last upright bar and draw up lp. There is same number of lps on hook as in Row 1.

Row 2—Second Half: Same as 2nd half of Row 1. Rep Row 2 until there are 18 rows from beg.

TO BIND OFF: Sk first 2 bars, loosely draw lp through next bar and through lp on hook (sl st), work sl st loosely in 2nd skipped bar, * sk next bar, sl st in next bar, sl st in sk bar; rep from *, ending sl st in last bar. Fasten off.

BORDER—NOTE: Work all sc through *back* lp of sts, all dc through *front* lp as described below and sk the sc directly behind the dc.

Rnd 1(worked through back lps only): With F hook from right side, join MC in first sl st at beg of bound-off row. Work 3 sc in same st with joining (corner), sc in each of next 23 sts, 3 sc in last st (corner); on next side edge (sc in *back* lp of st at end of each of next 2 rows, 2 sc in next st) 5 times, sc in each of last 3 sts—23 sc from corner; 3 sc in back lp of 2nd sc of foundation ch (corner), sc in horizontal st of next 23 chs, 3 sc in last ch (corner), work 23 sc on other edge to correspond. Join with a sl st to first sc. Break MC, draw C through lp on hook.

Rnd 2: Through back lp, sc in same st with joining, * 3 sc at corner, sc in each of 2 sc, sk 1 MC lp on edge of motif, (dc under next MC lp at edge, sk sc behind dc, sc in each of 3 sc, sk 3 MC lps on edge) 5 times, dc under next MC lp at edge, sk sc behind dc, sc in each of next 2 sc; rep from * on side, sk 2 MC lps instead of 3; work other 2 sides to correspond. 6 dc on each side. Join with a sl st to first sc. Break C, draw A through lp.

Rnd 3: Sc in same st with joining, * dc in center sc at corner of Rnd 1, 3 sc in corner st of Rnd 2, dc in same st as last dc, sk sc behind dc (sc in next st of Rnd 2, sk 1 st of Rnd 1, dc in next st of Rnd 1) 12 times, sc in next st of Rnd 2; rep from * around. Join with a sl st to first sc. Break A, draw B through lp.

Rnd 4: Dc in next sc of Rnd 2, sc in next dc of Rnd 3, * dc in center of sc of Rnd 2, 3 sc in center sc of Rnd 3, dc in same st with last dc (sc in next st of Rnd 3, dc in next st of Rnd 2) 13 times, sc in next st of Rnd 3; rep from * around. Join.

SIDE MOTIF (Make 10): With afghan hook and MC ch 32 to measure 9 inches.

Row 1: Same as Row 1 of Motif.

Row 2—First Half: Bind off first st, work pat to last 2 bars, insert hook under 2 bars, draw up 1 lp. 30 lps on hook. 1 st dec each side.

Row 2—Second Half: * Yo and draw through 2 lps; rep from * to last 2 bars (3 lps on hook), yo and draw through 3 lps. 1 st dec each side.

NOTE: Count number of lps on each row to be sure decs have been made and keep continuity of pat. Rep Row 2 twice. 20 sts. Be sure to work through only 1 bar where 2 are worked tog.

Row 5—First Half: Same as First Half of Row 2.

Row 5—Second Half: Same as 2nd Half of Row 1. Rep Row 5 until there are only 2 lps on hook after last dec row. Fasten off.

BORDER (side motif)—Rnd 1: With F hook from right side join MC in *back* lp of first ch of foundation ch, 3 sc in same place with joining (corner), sc in back lp of each of next 30 chs, 3 sc in last ch (corner, * leaving a lp at front, work 23 sc on edge, * 3 sc at point; rep between *'s once. Join with a sl st to first sc. Break MC, draw C through lp on hook.

Rnd 2: Sc in same st with sl st; 3 sc in next st, sc in each of 2 sts, sk 2 MC lps on motif, (dc in next lp, sk st behind dc, sc in each of next 3 sts) 6 times, sc in each of next 2 sts, dc in next st, sk 2 MC lps, sc in each of next 3 sts, 3 sc at corner, sc in each of next 3 sts, sk 2 MC lps, dc in next st, (sk sc behind dc, sc in each of 3 sts, dc in next lp) 4 times, sk st behind dc, sc in each of 2 sts, sk 2 MC lps, dc in next MC lp, sc in next st, 3 sc at corner, sc in next st, work 2nd side to correspond with dc's in matching rows. Join, break C, draw A through lp.

Rnds 3 and 4: Work as on Motif.

FINISHING: Block motifs and side motifs to measurements. Hold right side of motifs tog. With B and taking up top lp only of sts, matching sts, overcast motifs tog following diagram. With F hook and B, from right side through *back* lps work sc in each st, 3 sc at lower points on ends. Join with a sl st. Fasten off.

TASSELS (Make 8): Wrap all colors around a 7-inch cardboard and use 15 strands of each color.

TASSEL COVER Work with B. Draw MC strands at top of tassel through top of cover and using same strands, sew a tassel at each point on ends.

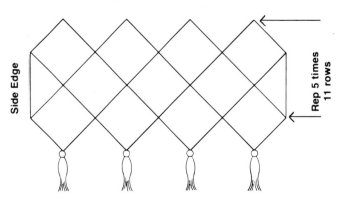

Lower Edge

Side Edge

Rep 5 times / 11 rows

Abbreviations

K	knit
P	purl
st	stitch
sk	skip
sl	slip
inc	increase
dec	decrease
tog	together
b	back
yo	yarn over
psso	pass sl st over
pat	pattern
beg	beginning
rep	repeat
rnd	round
MC	Main Color
CC	Contrast Color
dp	double point needle

St St	Stockinette St
ch	chain
sc	single crochet
dc	double crochet
tr	triple crochet
hdc	half double crochet
sp	space
lp	loop
grp	group
Tch	turning chain

To work even means to work without inc or dec.
* means repeat instructions following the * as many more times as specified, in addition to the first time.
( ) or [ ] means repeat the instructions enclosed in the parentheses as many times as indicated by the number immediately following.

Suggestions and Tips

Basic to the success of your afghan is your gauge, stitch gauge *and* row gauge. If these two integral ingredients are incorrect in relationship to the gauge given, your afghan will not measure the correct size. To determine your gauge, cast on or chain enough stitches to measure approximately 4 inches using the needles or crochet hook called for in the pattern. Work 4 inches and bind off. Using a tape measure and laying the swatch on a flat slick surface, count the number of stitches *and* rows in 4 inches. If in 4 inches your stitch and row gauge is MORE stitches to 1 inch than given in the directions, try the next size larger needle or crochet hook and again check your gauge. If your stitch and row gauge is LESS stitches to 1 inch than that given in the directions, try the next size smaller needle and again check your gauge. Remember, the needle or hook size used is not the most important matter, your gauge is.

When crocheting, unless stated in a set of instructions I have found these methods of increasing and decreasing to be most effective. When increasing in

single, half double, double and treble crochet, work 2 stitches in one stitch. When decreasing in single crochet, draw up a loop in each of next 2 stitches, yarn over and draw through 3 loops. In double crochet, (yarn over, draw up a loop in next stitch, yarn over and through 2 loops) 2 times—yarn over and through 3 loops. In treble crochet, yarn over 2 times, draw up a loop in next stitch, (yarn over and through 2 loops) 2 times—2 loops on hook; yarn over 2 times, draw up a loop in next stitch, (yarn over and through 2 loops) 2 times, yarn over and through 3 loops.

When knitting, there are several different increase methods available, and which one is best usually is determined by the pattern stitch and end result desired. However, when there is a pattern that just says "increase," I like this method best: Knit to the place of the increase, pick up the strand between stitches and knit this loop from the *back*. This gives a nice close increase with almost no hole. And one last word—enjoy!

Rosita S. McSwigan

Rosita S. McSwigan